Unexpected Jesus

Unexpected Jesus

The Gospel as Surprise

CRAIG HOVEY

 CASCADE Books • Eugene, Oregon

UNEXPECTED JESUS
The Gospel as Surprise

Copyright © 2012 Craig Hovey. All rights reserved. Except for brief quotations in critical publications or reviews, no part of this book may be reproduced in any manner without prior written permission from the publisher. Write: Permissions, Wipf and Stock Publishers, 199 W. 8th Ave., Suite 3, Eugene, OR 97401.

Scripture quotations are from the Revised Standard Version of the Bible, copyright © 1952 [2nd edition, 1971] by the Division of Christian Education of the National Council of the Churches of Christ in the United States of America. Used by permission. All rights reserved.

Chapter 5 includes a modified version of a previously published essay, used here by permission: "Is Your Resurrection Too Small?" *Theology* CXIII.873 (May/June 2010) 192–99.

Cascade Books
An Imprint of Wipf and Stock Publishers
199 W. 8th Ave., Suite 3
Eugene, OR 97401

www.wipfandstock.com

ISBN 13: 978-1-61097-879-8

Cataloging-in-Publication data:

Hovey, Craig, 1974–

    Unexpected Jesus : the gospel as surprise / Craig Hovey.

    x + 162 p. ; 23 cm. —Includes bibliographical references and index(es).

    ISBN 13: 978-1-61097-879-8

    1. Church and the world. 2. Christianity and culture. 3. Theology I. Title.

BV4638 .H68 2012

Manufactured in the U.S.A.

To my mother

He is a living God, and that means he is the God of surprise endings. He does this not because he takes malicious delight in toying with us, nor does he trap us to guffaw over the resulting pratfalls. The God of surprises is wholly righteous, wholly good, wholly just, wholly love, wholly light without a shadow of turning. He is faithful with the faithful, but the faithful throughout the centuries testify that God is a God of surprises. God surprises us because we have only the slightest grasp of what is actually going on in history or in our lives. God surprises us because he is doing far, far more than we can imagine, and his plans are far, far bigger than we can perceive.

—**Peter J. Leithart,** *1 & 2 Kings*

Come, thou long-expected Jesus.

—**Charles Wesley**

Contents

Preface ix
Introduction 1

1. Waiting with Intent 11
2. Staying Awake 31
3. Surprise Made Flesh 51
4. Free in Death 69
5. Jesus Christ in the Present Tense 82
6. Jesus the Stranger 98
7. Until He Comes 113
8. Theology and Surprise 133

Epilogue 147
Bibliography 153
Index 159

Preface

This book is meant to help the church find its way with a surprising God. It explores the curiosity of surprise as both a Christian reality and a theological category in its own right. It considers what it is like to live with the reality of a God and a gospel that do not cease to evoke in us wonder and astonishment.

There is at once a problem with even attempting to speak and write about surprise. Surely there cannot be much one can say without spoiling the surprise. There is only so much we can know about unknowing. But while this may rightly lead us to silence in the face of all that is unknown, we may also discern how to go on living in this way, a discernment to which we will devote words. The word Christians have for living in this way is *faith*.

Even so, our unknowing can also bring us the wrong kind of comfort. Following an unexpected God into a future that is in his hands more than ours may provoke our fear even while it can never be something to lament. Our wanting more of God is a salutary desire that is only stretched and deepened (and complicated and problematized) by our further experience of God. Nothing satisfies this longing other than a presence that will only serve to make us long more. But our desire for God can easily be a cover for other, less salutary desires, for esoteric knowledge, for special status to be used to reinforce human prejudice, for a more powerful advocate of positions we have already worked out. Our not knowing turns against all of these things, chastening our attempts to make God into an idol. But equally our refusal of idolatry can mask our more fundamental refusal to worship anything at all.

Preface

It occurs to me that Christians use both the language of faith and faith itself to walk the road that leads between these two. If we are tempted by certainty, then we may also be tempted to solidify our failure to achieve it into a reassuring principle. We may come to think that our inability to close in on what is true and real and certain disables the strivings of others as much as our own, and this perhaps to our great profit. This dialectic is well known under the headings of modernism and postmodernism. The false presence that modernity paraded as a knowledge has almost certainly been exactly inverted into an absence. Disbelief has, for some, a strange comforting quality. Crucially, though, it is still a knowledge, only now one that is a lack and so is tragically dependent on what comes before. What Christianity confesses—and it is surely easier to confess than to live—is a different kind of presence. More precisely, it is a different kind of dialectic of *both* presence *and* absence. The reason for this is that its chief concern is not with knowledge but with the *object*, what is simultaneously known and unknown. What does this mean? Modern and postmodern accounts of knowledge prioritize the ability to know something over the thing known (or unknown). Both are perilous.

I would like to express my thanks to Dr. Jason Fout for stimulating discussions as well as fruitful criticisms and provocations concerning an early draft. And since no single gesture can do justice to the years of unwavering support and encouragement I have received from my mother, I can only dedicate this book to her gratuitously and with love.

Introduction

There is an ambivalence that, by design, lies right at the heart of this book. I put it there in order to make sure that we wrestle with it, that we will not let go until we have done something with it—answered it, resolved it—or until it has defeated us. The reader will find a set of questions that revolve around an uncertainty, even a paradox, in our claims and abilities to know things. Is it possible to know something as new, surprising, and full of wonder without undoing all of these qualities?

For one thing, take God. Even while Christians believe and confess to know God, their act of opening themselves up to belief and knowledge means being available to what lies beyond what they now know and believe. They commit themselves, in their very act of believing, to being grasped by the object of their belief in ways that they do not foresee. If I choose to follow and trust a God whom I know, then how do I avoid merely tailoring that God to the limits of my knowledge? What is it like—and is it even possible—to commit myself to a God who still may act contrary to my expectations of who I thought this God was when I began? Does perhaps our knowing some things expose us in a new way to everything that is unknown? Does even what we thought we knew fall under this exposing? And if so, how do my knowing and exposing myself differ, if at all? Is our knowing God the same thing as our being open to God? Is God's freedom to act independently of our knowing him actually how we know him most genuinely and deeply?

These are difficult questions to answer. The reason has to do with the fact that Christianity takes knowing God to be fundamentally different from knowing other things. Consider that God has often revealed himself through promises. We come to know a God who makes himself known through acts that commit him to being the faithful God that he reveals himself to be. The thing promised only becomes knowledge so long as you believe that God is a faithful promise-maker, that he freely chooses in his promising to bind himself to what he promises to be and do. This knowledge is active faith that is kept alive with the constant work of maintaining trust. As this specific kind of knowledge, it surely disappears the moment that the promise-maker is rendered redundant, the content being somehow delivered in another way. The knowledge that "The LORD is slow to anger, and abounding in steadfast love, forgiving iniquity and transgression" (Num 14:18) is more than a deposit of information about the divine character; it is actual and true *as knowledge* as it is believed by a trust in the one who promises to be this way. Believing it does not make it true just as God's nature does not change depending on the vagaries of human confidence. But accounting these divine qualities as genuine knowledge of him involves the life of the knower with the life of God. Such involvement itself promises to be characterized by these things as much as God in himself (whatever that would mean). So it would surely be a mistake to separate too neatly who God is from what God promises to do. After all, knowing God as a faithful promise-maker—one who can be trusted to complete what he starts—is already a kind of knowledge of who God is. When it is revealed to Moses, God's very name (with the unusual grammar it implies) very closely associates God's being with God's faithfulness to be who he says he will be. One way to render the name that God reveals to Moses is "I will be who I will be" (Exod 3:14). By being God, God simply *is* a promise into the future; yet he is also himself the fulfillment of the promise that he makes. Which means that knowing God can be no more static than God's own movement between who God is and who he will be.[1]

Yet one obvious complication is this: the way that we know who God will be is never *for us* entirely captured by who we knew God to be when we decided to believe his promises. And the reason for this is precisely *because* God reveals himself in this specific way. God's presence to us (as to all of creation) is dynamic and living, and so it is something that we

---

1. Theologians have generally taken care to deny change in God. Usually this impulse is a good one—God is not *becoming* more faithful, for example—but sometimes it can mislead; emphasizing God's sameness can overwhelm our need to continue to look and long for, to struggle to recognize, how the manner of God fulfilling himself in different times and places is the same faithfulness as yesterday's.

can only know and have by being brought into its movement. We do not discover that God has changed, but that our knowledge of God grows commensurate with the living God.

Our lives are set in motion. Abram must leave Haran and journey to Canaan in order to discover that the God who promised to bless him speaks truthfully (Genesis 12). Abram changes his place and finds that God journeys with him. Jacob must return to the land that the Lord had promised to him and his ancestors in order to realize the truth of the Lord's promise to bring him back (Genesis 28). Only then does the graciousness of the covenant become supremely evident as itself a revelation of God's face (at *peniel*, "face of God," Gen 32:30), allowing Jacob to reconcile with the brother whom he had so wronged, saying "[I]f I have found favor in your sight, then accept my present from my hand; for truly to see your face is like seeing the face of God, with such favor have you received me" (Gen 33:10). The promise is revealed as true and trustworthy just as it is partially fulfilled to Jacob, who moves with (indeed wrestles with) the active God. Likewise with Jesus as the gospels portray him, particularly the Synoptic Gospels—actively on the move, at times frustratingly evasive, issuing the call to follow, as much to the church embodied in the women at the empty tomb as to the absent disciples (Mark 16:7). Even as raised from death, Christ has not "arrived" but, as ever, will only be known *as risen* by sharing in his life of movement and activity. In this book, I ask about what it is like to be able to say, "This isn't what I expected but I still know it is God." Or, perhaps better, to be able to say with Jacob, "Surely the LORD is in this place; and I did not know it" (Gen 28:16).

For at least two reasons (partly already intimated) it seems right to consider Jesus Christ in addressing these questions. First, it is a Christian conviction that Jesus Christ is God's definitive self-revelation. Jesus both fulfills promises made to Israel and issues new ones. Even though he is decisive and even in some sense *final*, Jesus does not bring to an end the difficulty of knowing the God whom he reveals. He does not, for example, deposit a new knowledge for us and then walk away; he does not leave behind, and in his place, a book of concluding and astonishing disclosures. We are expected to follow and, in our following, thereby know him. Jesus journeys into the unknown and bids us follow him there. It is not by accident that the motif of following has built into it movement, uncertainty, and even unpredictability. Second, the struggle within the gospels to identify Jesus as the Christ is a version of the struggle to be able to say,

Unexpected Jesus

"This isn't what I expected but I still know it is God." The qualities that the gospels want Christian disciples to develop—patience, hope, endurance, faithfulness—are ones that have this end in mind. What can we say about these qualities? How are they developed within us? For this, it is necessary to say something about how Christianity has spoken about the virtues.

I am deeply interested in how Christian convictions affect how Christians live. Within the theological tradition of which I am a part, the way of understanding how the living is linked to the believing is *indirect*. We are less often on the lookout for specific commands and directives. Rule-based ethics is incomplete and unsatisfying. We are more eager to discover how what we believe about God opens us to the changes that God enacts in us over time. This tradition emphasizes the virtues, dispositions (such as patience and generosity) that take a long time to increase in us and that are not generally achieved by directly aiming at them. When Christian theologians have built on the work of pagan virtue theorists like Aristotle, they have generally insisted that the goal of living—beatitude and friendship with God—is not a human achievement but a work of divine grace. St. Thomas Aquinas understood the most important virtues to be "infused" and, despite appearances perhaps, *gifts*.[2]

This is simply another way of saying that the virtues may even sneak up on us. It only occurs to us, after several years, that impatience and selfishness no longer have the hold on us that they once did. Where did they go? What has replaced them? The Christian virtues are surprising and unexpected. A spirit of gentleness, mercy, patience, and generosity makes sense after the fact; these qualities come together without our knowledge only to enable us to look back and see that where we have come to is a place that, until now, we did not know that we could reach.

I am intrigued by a few related qualities of the virtues along these lines. This is where ambivalence comes in again. On the one hand, virtues are not usually ends in themselves. What do I *do* if I want to become more patient or generous? The virtues are thus distinguished from so many self-help ideas, not so much in their substance (since self-help ideas

---

2. The reason for this is simply that Thomas identified the goal of living differently than did Aristotle. For Thomas, it is greater to be a participant and citizen of God's city than of earthly cities. To be fit for the former, one "must be elevated by the grace of God. For it is manifest that the virtues that are man's as a participant in this city cannot be acquired by him through his natural powers; hence they are not caused by our acts but are infused in us as a divine gift." Aquinas, *Disputed Questions on Virtue*, 57–58.

also intend to make us better people). Rather they are distinguished in their method. Even while we speak about the virtues as being extremely important, they only really work as virtues when subordinated to something else that surpasses them—whatever projects or activities or crafts or practices to which we have become so devoted that in the course of doing them, we cannot help being changed into more efficient practitioners. The virtues merely name the ways we have become more efficient.

But efficient at what? There is, after all, a sense of motion in even our conception of what the good is—the thing toward which we are directed—since our knowing it increasingly becomes an *experiential* knowledge the closer we get to it. We may have wanted to become more of this or that character trait, but without the overriding activity, we will probably not have what it takes to grow in the virtues. No one takes up a sport with the intention of developing the virtue of sportsmanship; or if they do, as a reason for engaging in it, it will prove insufficient for attaining that virtue. Sportsmanship is acquired because it is a requirement for attaining excellence at the sport. In fact, talking about "what it takes" is only a different way of invoking virtue-language.[3] Yet there is a circle that remains closed to us if we try to break through it directly. Straightforward efforts to increase my own patience or humility, for example, are more likely to provide me with plenty of practice in irritability and self-fascination than to encourage their opposites.[4] The twentieth-century Anglican moral theologian Kenneth Kirk argued that the way of Christian virtue is opaque to strategies that are either overly formal (and therefore easy to evade) or are preoccupied with the rigors of their own moral strivings. Both, Kirk adduced, fail to be led by the vision of God and God's kingdom to which the most appropriate response is not so much *morality* as *worship*.[5] Worship directs us away from ourselves and toward God in a movement that opens the way for Christian virtue.

---

3. The Greek for virtue, *areté*, is simply an excellence that we might characterize as "what it takes" to do something excellently, determined by whatever activity it is. See Plato, *Republic*, 352d–353e.

4. In an essay that claims Augustine for his own concept of Christian realism, Reinhold Niebuhr notes a "paradox of self-realization through self-giving" internal to the Christian gospel: "For the kind of self-giving which has self-realization as its result must not have self-realization as its conscious end; otherwise the self by calculating its enlargement will not escape from itself completely enough to be enlarged." Niebuhr, "Augustine's Political Realism," 137.

5. Kirk, *Vision of God*.

So the only way into the virtues, it seems, is by another route. It will have to be indirect and embarked upon with the expectation that there is more to this route than what it appears to be at first—its payoff, if you like, will exceed my initial aims and goal-setting. If I take up an activity with the hope of acquiring a virtue or two that will enable me to do it well, I will inevitably discover a surplus of effects that had not been included in my original goal. This discovery is actually the virtues at work. Increasing in some virtues will mean that I now act in the world differently and see it with altered vision. I have affected not just my orientation to the activity, but my orientation to just about everything else. Aristotle noted that there is a unity to the virtues—it is probably not possible to become more temperate and moderate while also not becoming more patient and humble, or to become more courageous without also becoming more honest.[6] While I will have to be more captivated by the activity than the virtues I hope to acquire if I ever hope to acquire them, I will also need to be open to the *more*—the unexpected things—that come with committing myself to my convictions.

One question that triggered this book simply has to do with the nature of this indirectness. How ought we to understand any knowledge that exceeds itself in its effects? What can be said about Christian convictions and beliefs that are simultaneously open to being surprised by more than they can anticipate once they devote themselves to being expressed in living?

In what follows, I undertake to develop a theology of Jesus Christ according to the idiom of surprise. I mean for it to be an exercise in primary theology. Rather than presenting an exhaustive account of a topic, I explicate a theological perspective using one particular lens in hopes that something significant in itself may result, perhaps drawing attention to neglected elements.

Because the theme is surprise, much of what is said here concerns a theology about the future. If movement is a fundamental characteristic

---

6. For Aristotle, the reason for the unity of the virtues lies in one having *phronesis*, which, as a "single state," entails having all of the virtues as well. See *Nicomachean Ethics*, 1145a.

of knowing something, then we must reckon with a future that is not easily pictured, that resists being known ahead of schedule because it is not determined by us. The future is the time of surprise when we do not expect it. It is how we experience the reality that it exists beyond our control. We are, after all, creatures for whom God's future is also our own. Our knowing it, even our speaking about it, always occurs in the time within which this future will come. Living into such a future is something that Christians believe can be done, despite everything else, with patience and hope. Two comments are in order, points that will be further explored later on.

First, the future of the created order is bound up with the future of Jesus Christ. What happens to all of us, the generations that will follow on after our deaths, the other creatures, and the inanimate cosmos—all of this Christians affirm somehow to be enfolded within the life of Jesus. This is actually as extraordinary a claim as it sounds (and will be looked at in depth in what follows). Second, the life of Jesus Christ is now. Christian theology has notoriously tied itself into knots attempting to explain how it is that the good news about Jesus is both now and to come, how what we affirm about the difference Jesus makes to the way things are is nevertheless incomplete, that it awaits something further. A difficulty is that we might be forgiven for wondering whether Jesus' cry from the cross—"It is finished!" (John 19:30)—really speaks the truth. If the cross is a victory over death and the powers of this world, for example, why do we still die and why do they still kill us? This side of the cross and resurrection, what more are we waiting for?

The *more*, as I allude to it, is the key to hopeful expectation, of not prematurely foreclosing on the expectations we feel are authentically generated by God's work in and among the church. God gives more of himself than we recognize or know what to do with. Yet it would be a mistake to think that the *more* is somehow a function of God's absence, that (as it is sometimes put) between the resurrection (or ascension) of Jesus and his final return at the end of time, we exist either partly or wholly abandoned, made to suffer a tragic existence where suffering continues and is even possibly made worse by our having been told news that, while it promises good, every indication is really otherwise—everything seems instead to point to it not yet being wholly for us.

Much of that, without doubt, is true. To be human means that we cannot escape being subject to the ravages of history except through death. And even then are we not still, in some sense, history's victims? What we leave behind in death, the loves from which we are separated, are in time. "It is finished" does not signal the end of this connection between human living and history. The difference it signals is that the history of the world and of the church that now lives a perilous existence is not perilous because God has left it to be so; it is no less perilous but for the fact that God's presence to it continues to be the life of Jesus. God's life with his creatures *in Christ* is not only the way that God shares history with us; it is also the way that, as historic beings, we share in God. Put differently, Jesus' itinerant preaching in first-century Palestine is no more his *life*—in every sense of the word—than his risen fellowship with and in and as the church as a risen body.

There is little use pretending that this solves everything or makes matters more bearable for Christians. But it should discipline and clarify the nature of our waiting. If I may be allowed to play with our language slightly, I suggest we think in terms, not of waiting *for* Jesus or *for* God to act, but in terms of our waiting finding itself *within* Jesus' present life and *within* God's hiddenness, not as absence, but as unseen presence. The great Christian mystics often speak about God's presence as a mystery, ill-defined, more like fire or a cloud than a list or a statue.[7] We might have just as many reasons to call God's mysterious *here-ness* an absence rather than a presence. It is in the character of mysteries to draw us in without fully revealing themselves; they entice without giving themselves away in the process. This cuts against the grain of modern existence, which soothes itself with the knowledge that anything worth knowing must be knowable, hence confidently being able to draw a clear line between those things that are rational and those things that are not, or between the things that will and will not stand up to scrutiny. It seemed that mystery was easily dispelled, but not because it was exposed and converted to patent and consumable knowledge. Rather, it was dispelled by a form of inquiry and commensurate ways of living that discouraged interest in it. Still, for many, such interest did not completely die.

---

7. The fourteenth-century tract *The Cloud of Unknowing* is a good example ("By love may He be gotten and holden; but by thought never," ch. 6), although Gregory of Nyssa also makes much of this image in *The Life of Moses*. Indeed, Denys Turner notes that postmodern philosophy has paved the way for mystery to make a comeback ("The Darkness of God and the Light of Christ").

Introduction

Paradoxically enough, I began thinking through the themes of this book by considering a series of emphatic claims about Jesus, claims that over time it seemed appropriate to subject to the reality about Jesus that they claim: he is living, free, raised from death. If these are true things that ought to be said of him, then the ways they are held as knowledge ought to conform to what they claim. In short, can unexpectedness and surprise ever be for us forms of knowing anything? How does theology respond to a God who insists on acting before us in these ways as very entailments of the divine? I wanted seriously to consider the joyous presence of Christ in the world as also an unfathomable one, a life that continues to hold forth promise and anticipation just as it enjoins and confirms the trust and belief that make these things possible.

In the following chapters, I try to do justice to these topics and questions. In particular, I am interested in the kinds of things that make Jesus surprising—that keep him appropriately *unknown* and *unexpected* to us. Most obvious is simply the confession that he is now living, having been raised by the Father. As a living person, he acts in the present tense by being present to the church in a relation that cannot fully be anticipated. This is normal for all of our relationships with living people. That we cannot now see him disables every way that we would make our seeking into forms of grasping at him. In fact, Jesus is most fully himself when he speaks to us out of his hiddenness from us. As we shall see, this hiddenness need not be a form of distance but may in fact be the most genuine form of disclosure.[8]

In these pages, I continually loop through a process of making Jesus more strange rather than familiar, of generating a right and proper distance between Christian existence and the existence of Jesus Christ for the purpose of practicing the kind of encounter with him that I believe the New Testament goes to great lengths in order to preserve for its readers. I refer to this process and this looping back as attempts to "un-expect" Jesus. Theology must always seek to transcend its present formulations in the confidence that God will not be exhaustively known or mastered by

---

8. "[E]verything that we might perhaps say about it can be said only in face of this truth, only as we stand by it, namely, the truth that also and precisely in his revelation God is the hidden God.... Those who do not know the revealed God, what do they know of the hidden God?... God is hidden then, not because of the relativity of all human knowledge, but because he is the living God who reveals himself as he is, the triune God, inexhaustibly living, immutably the subject, from himself and not from us" (Barth, *Göttingen Dogmatics*, 135).

fixed horizons. According to David Bentley Hart, theology is therefore "always unmoored, capable of disrupting stable hierarchies of interpretation, of inspiring endless departures and returns."[9]

Yet I do not mean to confuse a healthy un-expectation with either apathy or a kind of dogmatic agnosticism. I mean more authentically to associate it with the possibility of being surprised. If one is apathetic about whether something arrives or not (a letter in the post, say), then one obviously does not expect it. But one also is not likely to be too surprised by it if it ever happens to turn up. Instead, what I hope to get at is a salutary form of expectation that is active and open to being alarmed and surprised.

The body of the book comprises eight chapters that are meant roughly to correspond to key elements and demands of the gospel. The first two chapters look at the Christian dispositions of what I call "un-expectation"—waiting for Jesus with Advent and Lenten faith (chapter 1) and being watchful and awake (chapter 2). Next follow three chapters about moments in the gospel narrative: the Incarnation of Jesus (chapter 3), the Cross (chapter 4), and the Resurrection (chapter 5). Chapter 6 begins to show some concrete implications of the account of Jesus set forth in the preceding chapters. Through the prism of asking about the nature of Jesus' difference from us, it explores friendship and children (including adult friendships with children other than our own). Chapter 7 looks at the hope for Christ's return by asking how Christians ought to think about, and live in light of, the Day of the Lord. A brief survey of the Bible on this theme, especially in the Prophets, culminates in a consideration of the surprised ones of Matthew 25 ("Lord, when did we see you . . . ?"). The chapter concludes by showing how the Eucharist both models and instantiates an appropriate presence and absence for the church as Christ's body. Chapter 8 turns finally to the topic of theology itself by asking how theology should be conducted in the face of a God capable of surprises. It considers pitfalls by which theology is tempted to latch onto objects other than God. The concluding Epilogue is a sermon that highlights the book's central themes in the mode of proclamation.

---

9. Hart, *Beauty of the Infinite*, 19.

chapter one

Waiting with Intent

Come, thou long-expected Jesus.

The opening line from Charles Wesley's 1744 hymn directs us toward the great Christian theme of hope. It prompts us to play off our hoping against our wanting, even against our impatience. The words are a cry for help, imploring Jesus to put an end to our waiting and fulfill our hopes. It is invitation and a heartfelt summons. It is like the psalmist whose prayer has become the cry of Israel and the church: "How long must I bear pain in my soul, and have sorrow in my heart all the day? How long shall my enemy be exalted over me?" (Ps 13:2). The final words of the New Testament express the same sentiment (Rev 22:20), as though the Bible itself has put in the hard work for the sake of the church only now to help it remain faithful until the time when Jesus will arrive in glory. The people formed by the Bible—both as the lives that produced it so long ago and as the lives that it has made possible since then—have received a lot that is good at the hand of God. But they have not received everything that they ultimately need.

Waiting is extremely hard, and its difficulty is probably in proportion to the desire we feel. It also generates some interesting questions. For instance, is it easier to wait for something that is important or is it harder? If we are honest, we would probably have to admit that it is both. We are more likely to persist—to keep waiting—when we have to wait for something that is truly life-changing. On the other hand, if it is something we could take or leave, that we do not really care all that deeply about in the first place, then waiting for it will not be that hard. But in situations like this, we are also likely to wonder what all the fuss is about and to move on to other things.

Why *should* we have to wait for Jesus? The sons and daughters of Israel waited a long time for a messiah. Now that he has come, though, waiting for him to come back probably strikes many Christians as doubly counterintuitive, if not entirely unnecessary. After all, is not part of the Christian message—the Christian joy, in fact—that Jesus did not really leave? Yes, he ascended to the Father, but his Spirit returned at Pentecost, enflamed the apostles, created the church, and inspired them to engage in the church's mission to all people. And not only this, Christians throughout the ages have spoken of the "presence" of Jesus in many ways. They have discovered love and comfort in his closeness, and a great number have spoken about Jesus as sacramentally present in the Eucharist. So the very suggestion that Christians are waiting for Jesus might very well generate its own impatience.

More to the point, it is worth asking whether Christians really know what we are asking and waiting for when we say we wait for Jesus. What makes us think that we would recognize him if he just showed up unannounced, which is what he says he will do (Matthew 24)? What would be the point of waiting and hoping for one who himself haunts us with the possibility that we will miss him when he comes? What does this say about our hoping after all? Are we, for example, more likely to recognize Jesus if we get our hopes right? Will our expecting him lead us to see him? In the first century, those who failed to recognize Jesus for who he was—Israel's Messiah—did not suffer, by and large, from the problem of *not expecting* a messiah. They did not fail to hope that they would be delivered (although many also clearly *did* fail to hope in this way). Instead, what they expected differed from who and what Jesus actually was. Even Peter's confession that Jesus is the Christ (Matthew 16, Mark 8) is immediately followed by an episode in which Peter makes clear that he really doesn't know what a Christ is, that he has no intention of allowing Jesus to go through with the unavoidable future that he sees for himself. If Peter is to be remembered as much for his misunderstanding as for his correct answer about Jesus' identity (in Mark, Jesus does not even congratulate Peter for his right answer), then we ought to treat his reaction as a great Christian danger and temptation.

Waiting with Intent

Let us characterize the danger and temptation as having to do with presumption and knowledge. It is the presumption that we know Jesus Christ, that he fits easily within our understanding, and that he conforms to an idea we might have—perhaps a great and exalted idea called "Christ" or "Christology"—but an idea nonetheless. I will address this way of *knowing* Jesus as at once a danger and a temptation since it can really ultimately be a way of avoiding the hard work of coming to know him as he really is. Christologies become a problem when they are taken to provide sufficient accounts of who Christ is. At their best, Christianity's most important descriptions of who and what Jesus is (such as descriptions of his two natures) actually go on to raise as many questions as they answer for those who confess them to be true. If the new questions are not asked, it is difficult to see how the answers to the previous ones are doing the work they are meant to. For many who first encountered Jesus, their expectation was flawed for perhaps not also being a *longing* as it should have been. It was not a genuine need. Or, perhaps better, what the Pharisees and others who rejected Jesus truly wanted and needed was not something the Messiah genuinely brings. And so is this not a problem? It seems to me that it should be a concern for all Christians who confess an expectation for Jesus.

The ones on whose side the gospel most clearly declares itself to be are more likely to welcome Jesus because of how he satisfies their longing—the poor are blessed and the good news is brought to them (Luke 6:20; 4:18). Could it be that the expectation that the poor will be blessed is more fundamental to our ability to discover Jesus among the poor (and hence to discover him *at all*, if that is truly where he will be found) than the sum total of human effort to correct our seeing by more direct methods? Could it be that the drive to try to see clearly is actually disabled in proportion to its success when it commits itself only to a general strategy in which Jesus is merely one object among many? Consider a parallel from Greek philosophy.

In one of the well-known Socratic dialogues by Plato, Socrates' interlocutor, Meno, objects that it seems we can never truly learn anything new; no new knowledge is possible. The reason he gives is this: In order to begin to search for something, you must know what it is you are searching for. How else would you know when you have found it and therefore know to stop your search? Yet if you already know what you are searching for, there is no reason to set about searching for it. This kind of objection is meant to complicate the ways that we think about learning something—can there ever be genuine learning of anything? The ultimate self-flatterer denies that he has anything else to learn beyond what he already knows. But perhaps what we call learning something can also be an extended exercise in self-flattery, a drawn out series of games we engage in by which we tell ourselves that we are improving ourselves, all the while applying to ourselves the very standard we also use to determine what is "new" to us when none of it actually is. Perhaps it even serves the complicated task of flattering ourselves into believing that we are not the kinds of self-flatterers who think they already know it all.

Who are you satisfying when you close your mind on something new, finding and judging it to be right and genuine? It is only yourself, it seems. But if so, then are you not already the one who possesses the standard of judgment *ahead of your encounter* with what you are calling "new"? Socrates has little patience for this so-called Meno paradox. He complains that thinking of this kind makes us lazy and that people with idle minds (rather than energetic ones) like to hear it.[1] Having disabused ourselves of the drive and need to search after things, having succeeded in convincing ourselves that they are things that we already have, then there can be nothing we genuinely lack. While we may feel as though our knowledge could be increased, what we know and do not know already constrain us from achieving anything like it. Why not rather rest, having made peace with our limitation? The link between work and knowledge is broken and the human mind, thus released from intellectual labor and the self-generated servitude to which it had grown used to surrendering, is now given over to the repose of the satisfied mind.

It is worth noticing what the Meno paradox assumes. For one thing, it excludes that class of things whose value is closely associated with the desire one must have in order to seek after them. There are things that I want *because* I have knowledge of them, not because my knowledge is lacking. But knowing them is not enough to make them something that I "have." Consider love. On the one hand, it is necessary to know something about what love is in order to recognize it when you encounter and experience it. But we also say that someone who "does not know the meaning of love" lacks more than knowledge. Love is not something that I can "have" just by knowing about it; but just as surely we suspect that you

---

1. Plato, *Meno*, 81e.

cannot really know it without having it. Just so, one who loves can be said to "know" the meaning of love more deeply and genuinely the more he is aware that love transcends knowledge. And the situation never actually threatens to resolve itself as an act of knowing—the lover who responds to the frustration that love exceeds knowing by merely trying to *know* more without trying to *love* more, will in fact end up both knowing and loving less, and both for precisely the same reason. Instead, love produces in the lover a deeper desire for more love, together with the full awareness that this requires a bona fide seeking that will never give up for being overfull, but only for being satisfied with too little.

This interplay between love and knowledge differs markedly from the Meno paradox, even though it is also a paradox. At the least it indicates that there are different kinds of knowledge. And perhaps the kinds that are most highly to be prized are those that shift most markedly in their relationship to us as we pursue them. Or, slightly differently, our pursuing them is an activity that refashions our desire to know. This is why knowing a person is so different from knowing an idea. The more I know a person, the less I am able to make them function as an object of mine; when I know them though love, this is ever more the case.

I have developed a lesson from Socrates and Meno in my own way, but I think it helps us understand what we mean when we say that Christianity confesses Christ to be much more than an idea. He is a person who can be spoken of as present and living. He does not merely call disciples from the page of the text, but journeys with them in life—theirs and his. The life they share is essential to how he is known by those who dare to let the life of Jesus define their own (Gal 2:20).

Yet Jesus is present to the world in a complex way, or at least in a manner unique among other things that are present and the manner of their being present to us. If something is present to me, it is available and is not something for which I must wait. No other person who is fully present—at least in the ways that we normally think of—also promises to *come back*. Such promising is neither necessary nor comprehensible. Jesus' presence, in this sense, must also be an absence. This is one reason Christianity has often sought to describe Jesus Christ with us *sacramentally*—he is present to and even, in some sense, *as* the church, his body, while he is also the *head* of the church, which is his bride. His presence is known as a presence when it is believed as the promise that it is. In a distinction common to a great deal of eucharistic theology, Christ's promise to be present *to* and *among* us is available only to the eyes of faith and not to our five senses.

Therefore, let us speak of two dimensions of Jesus' presence and absence. On one axis lies time. Jesus is present in both the present and future tenses. Who he is to and for us *now* is real, yet also different from who he *will be* when God is "all in all." Our present is neither properly despair—as though God had not in fact given us Christ—nor a reason not to hope for more of him. The present and future dimensions are related such that his present presence is responsible for the impulse to await and long for all that is absent about him, even while the absence is not entirely unknown to us, lest we worry that we do not know what we are waiting for and will not be able to recognize it when it comes. This is the axis of time.

On the other axis lies material existence. Jesus' presence with the world is *as something*, which is to say in some form that is one with the world by being part of it. The incarnate Christ does not merely reside in the world as an outsider, but is born to the world by sharing its nature. Much of the early debate surrounding the personhood of Jesus Christ centered on how we ought to talk about his identity as one who is at once a creature and uncreated, human and divine, at one with us in our material existence and above all materiality. The task of resolving these tensions is probably no easier than that which is involved in addressing those regarding time. We inhabit several paradoxes when we commit ourselves to talking about Christ with care. Our refusal to resolve these tensions prematurely may also be a way of signaling Christ's uniqueness and our decision to keep from knowing him in any ways that would make him less than he actually is. Christ's and our material existence is the second axis. In both cases—with time and with matter—Christ's presence and absence are potentially full of surprise.

We should not ignore the fact that it is altogether possible to *want* to be surprised. This may come from an awareness that we are very often the ones who exert the most powerful limitations on our own experiences. We require surprise in order truly to be broken out of ruts and routines, since we are too reluctant to initiate genuine change on our own. Often the best we can summon is the will to be overwhelmed by something that we know we lack the will to choose.

Waiting with Intent

Even at these times, though, do we not want to be surprised more by some things than by others? A lover of a certain style of music may enlist the Internet for discovering new music, for being surprised by an unknown playlist. But surprise is seldom absolute. Without some acquaintance with the thing that surprises, it is very difficult to see how it could surprise at all, how responding in surprise is appropriate to its newness to me. The appearance of something that in no way connects with what I have known or have experienced will not elicit my response by which I reveal the contradictions with my knowledge and experiences. If I know the way things typically go, then I will be most surprised by things that go a different way. But this difference cannot be absolute; if it were, I would not see the different way of going as a way of going whatsoever.

The United States' saber-rattling prior to the 2003 invasion of Iraq included a deliberate propaganda campaign that warned of impending military "shock and awe" to be released upon Baghdad. Why talk about the shock ahead of time? Does not anticipating a shock lessen its severity when it comes? Does it not mitigate the disorientation it is meant to cause? No doubt the Defense Department had their reasons, but I suspect that part of it discloses the reality of how we recognize something as shocking, as surprising. Surprise is not entirely opposed to knowledge—it does not have the pure form of what one does not know. When confronted by something I do not know, so long as it does not too radically challenge too much of what I *do* know, I will simply learn it. The more readily I am able to make what I learn "fit" with things I have already learned, the more quickly and confidently I will domesticate its newness, particularly as it will ratify my rightness in some respects; by definition, I am less likely to be surprised by it.

Why then would I *want* to be surprised by some things? Let us suppose, first of all, that I do *not* genuinely want to be surprised, or that what appears to be this desire is not authentic. Perhaps I feign being surprised by what only benignly sanctions everything about which I already want to believe that I am right. How surprising, I might say, that I turned out to be right all along without knowing it! (In *Meno*, Socrates makes much of the distinction between truly knowing something and simply having a "correct opinion" about it.) Yet disingenuousness aside, I am merely showing that what I claimed not to "know" has now surprised me by suddenly becoming, for me, a knowledge. But it should be obvious that I will only recognize it as knowledge to the extent that it is something I already have, which is to say that it cannot actually be a surprise. I may be pleased by a discovery, but it seems it may only be a surprising one if it is decidedly *not* something that I already had.

There is clearly a tension. On the one hand, in order to work, surprise must "fit" with things that do not surprise. This is necessary in order to recognize it as a contrast. Things that share *nothing* in common can hardly be said to clash with each other. But on the other hand, the greater the fit, the less surprising it will be. Have we come to the seemingly unpromising conclusion that "surprise" is some kind of middle ground between what is completely known (if there is ever such a thing) and the completely unknown? I do not think so, for to know something as "in the middle" is yet a further deadening of what might otherwise be surprising. But how would we ever know that we are in the middle without knowing the two poles from which we are equidistant?

Even so, can we *ever* be truly surprised? Or do we always risk undercutting the very thing that we desire through our precise desiring of it? Perhaps the way that the "shock and awe" propaganda campaign preceded the acts they were anticipating illustrates a deeper dimension at work in these things. Could it be that our inability to prepare for those things about which we have partial knowledge, unable to convert them to full knowledge, is in fact part of the disorientation of the surprise itself? Put differently, is it possible that, rather than mitigating shock that might otherwise accompany what we easily see as a more authentic element of surprise, the destabilization begins earlier—in thinking, in fear, in anticipation? The standard account of America's campaign is to declare that the actual invasion "shocked" far less than we expected (and it goes without saying that who the "we" is matters deeply here), partly on account of how the surprise had been spoiled. Expectations had been raised too high. Yet I suspect that any correspondence between the forecast and its fulfillment was incidental. The greatest expressions of fear and awe probably come about gradually rather than suddenly. A people must learn to cower in the face of threats that may or may not fulfill themselves so long as the generation of fear is considered to be the most fundamental goal. After all, a fearful people may simply police themselves, crumble rather than fight back. What does this suggest about our wanting to be surprised?

One thing it means is not only that what we know enlarges the set of things untouched by that knowledge, but also that knowing some things also increases our capacity for surprise. I suggest that this is because knowing is a clumsy way of suspecting that we might overcome being surprised by other things—clumsy because our sense of omniscience will always outpace the reality. Our experience of surprise thus witnesses to what is incomplete about our knowing.[2] If so, then our overreaching through knowing and knowledge is not only a way of preparing ourselves in order to avoid the possibility that we will be surprised. It is actually part of our actual response to the wonder, or rather our refusal to wonder appropriately. Conversely, if there is a salutary "wanting to be surprised," it may arise out of having come to a better appreciation for our limits as knowers.

My knowledge and my drive for converting more of reality into knowledge is something of which I may become aware and lament, though I may simultaneously lack the ability to overcome it without falling into some of the paradoxes I have been describing here. I may know that my knowing never adequately reduces reality to my possession without remainder while also suspecting that I will need to depend on something beyond my control to break through to me. Reality's "remainder" can only come to me, in a sense, on its own, under its own power, and within its own categories, if it is to be "more" to my knowing it.[3] My wanting it to surprise me will thus by needs exceed my knowing in advance what it is that I want to be surprised by. Yet it will genuinely be a surprise so long as I have come to hold what I know with a humility appropriate to what I *also* "know" to be the excessiveness of things, even while I do not know these things in their excessiveness.

When God surprises, it is often by providing a way out of the present circumstance that is neither self-evident nor flows mechanistically from the givens of the situation. It is a supremely ethical conviction when Christians refuse to choose between what appear to be the only available

---

2. And it is, to be sure, a particular kind of knowing. Robert W. Jenson writes that "there must be vastly more of reality that is intrinsically hidden from our research than is available to it" (*Canon and Creed*, 102).

3. Jean-Luc Marion speaks about the concept of the saturated phenomenon in this way—something presents itself to me but exceeds and overwhelms my grasp; I can no more anticipate it than be equipped with the concepts and categories with which to comprehend and contain it. Marion discusses this concept in several works, including "The Saturated Phenomenon," 177–216.

options. John Howard Yoder discusses Johannes Hamel, a pastor in communist East Germany, who frequently wondered how Christians ought to live under such a regime. Should they make an issue of honesty and faith or should they lie low and suffer with patience the system of injustice? Assuming that Christians must be honest about the way that the world is and the way that they find it, Hamel writes: "Time and again God creates loopholes, open space in the midst of closed systems of unbelief and hatred of God. Here the possibility is offered and realized for doing the good, reasonable, and well-pleasing, although these systems theoretically seem to leave no room for such action."[4]

Hamel diagnoses our inability to be surprised by the God of the gospel. It stems from a reliance on life as a closed system, of disbelief grounded in those things that are theoretical possibilities. But why should we trust theories about what is possible in view of the Christian proclamation that God has promised to do what is impossible in order to secure for humanity a way out of sin and death? And if God has already acted impossibly in Jesus Christ, Christianity has every reason to expect such actions again and again. Hamel continues:

> Where people take their place in this self-movement of the Gospel, there opens, *usually by surprise*, a door by which they can get on in their earthly life. To be sure most of the time this door is only visible in the last moment. One must have enough faith to run against a doorless wall up to the last centimeter, in the certain hope that God who leads one in this way will not allow his people to break their heads . . . More than once we have believed ourselves to be finished . . . Then in the last minute God stepped in and made it clear to us, so clear that we were ashamed of ourselves, so that he only needs to move a little finger to make things come out quite otherwise than we could have foreseen.[5]

Perhaps there is a paradox in the kind of living and knowing that makes it more likely to expect God's surprises. After all, if you expect to be surprised in one particular way or another, you will not be surprised at all, since you will have converted what is an unknown impossibility into something that is on the same horizon with other possible things. Yet it is the absoluteness of that horizon that itself must be called into question by a people whose living is to testify to the reality of God's unexpected care

4. Cited in Yoder, *What Would You Do?*, 33.
5. Cited in ibid., 33–34, emphasis added.

Waiting with Intent

for the world and rescue of sinners. These are situations, places, and times in which the Christian's faith witnesses to the belief that God has resolved to act, to bring a way out of what appears to be a closed set of options. "Does not the Christian belief in resurrection—not simply as one bygone event but as God's pattern of action in human experience—mean that it is precisely where we do not see how a situation can possibly be worked out that God might demonstrate his saving intent? Precisely because it is he who must act I cannot suggest how that might be."[6] Yoder makes use of Hamel's account in order to answer the question that pacifists face from those who ask what you should do if confronted with an act of aggression and the "only" way out lies in the use of violence in response. Miracle or surprise quickly take the discussion beyond the usual parameters for an ethics based on tough cases. Yoder objects to the way that the question presupposes the correct answer; he developed a reputation for refusing to accept certain kinds of questions along these lines. In my view, one of the most important responses to the question of violence has to do with martyrdom. "The New Testament and much later Christian testimony indicate that martyrdom is in some sense a normal path for at least some Christians to need to follow at least sometimes. How then could I possibly be led along the path of innocent suffering if my pragmatic managing of the 'what if . . . ?' situation determines this as the one thing I must not let happen?"[7] Martyrdom may not look much like a "way out" of a troublesome ethical dilemma, but by being a way of sharing in the way that God shares himself with the world, it can be a faithful response to a situation in which the only way out is through death to resurrection, as it indeed was for Jesus. Yoder's arguments along these lines show, I think, that the discipline of Christian ethics has been slow to consider the moral seriousness of how victims may yet act in the faith that God is the primary one who acts.[8] The paradox lies in simultaneously trusting that God will act to fulfill the divine promises while also admitting ignorance of how this might happen. It is therefore the central dynamic of a living faith.

The impossibility of God's action in the gospel continues to repeat itself so long as it really continues to be a true story. It is a profound characteristic of this particular story that its truth is so counterintuitive that

---

6. Ibid., 34.
7. Ibid., 40.
8. My own attempt to think with some care along these lines is Hovey, *To Share in the Body*.

it can only be known through a people who are determined to live as though it is true.[9] They witness to the possibility of things that are extremely unlikely and that no amount of scrupulous dialectic or careful reasoning will on their own conclude. If there exist no people who claim that their living is made possible by such things, then whatever truth they might otherwise have, they cannot have the truth of what Christians mean by the good news. This immediately thrusts the church to the fore as an agent in God's revelation of this news to the world. Under such conditions, any information about Christianity might amuse hearers or notify those who listen of some facts about historical events. But there will not be proclamation. If the gospel moves, as Hamel says, by opening invisible doors—if it advances by *surprise*—then it can only really be true when it genuinely does so. The report that it is surprising will only be a true report if it is a surprising one.

The gospel forever confronts a world whose unbelief in God is nurtured by its more determined convictions about limited options and meager possibilities. For the world to move from unbelief to faith, from rebellion to submission, God mounts a continual confrontation of surprises against it. Most surprising of all, though, is God's recruitment of the church in doing so. Paul understood his own conversion in these terms; God not only surprised Paul on the Damascus road, but Paul's Christianity became God's surprise to the church. This means that integral to the church's mission is not only its ability to come to terms with a God who is determined to surprise it. It is also the facility for living with uncertainty—not that God will not again surprise, but that God remains God and is surprise's true source. What is the manner of this living? How can this people's expectation in a God of surprise keep from hardening into the kind of knowledge that, at best, cannot help witnessing to a false god, if not a dead one?

The church celebrates through anticipation during two seasons: Advent and Lent. It is important to emphasize that Lent does not anticipate the resurrection of Christ but instead looks through the darkness toward

---

9. The "as though" drops away the moment one genuinely believes it to be true. We should say that we here have a people whose determination is to *live its truth*.

the crucifixion. As Holy Week steps through the events of Jesus' Passion, the cross seems inevitable. We know it is coming. However, the risen Christ is not the object of Lenten waiting, for the resurrection is to remain an utter surprise. It is the unforeseeable and unknowable arrival of something that is completely unexpected. Christians deny themselves the joy of Easter until Easter itself comes. This leaves the resurrection to be an eminently *Advent* event. It resembles the object of hope that the church embodies as an Advent church, hoping for something that will still always surprise us, longing for the arrival of something that will exceed our longing, yet not in a manner for which we can prepare. In the words of Adrienne von Speyr, "For anyone who excludes hope from his faith, that faith becomes closed knowledge."[10]

I intend for the word *unexpected* to do work in a double sense. Most straightforwardly, I intend a theological point about Jesus—that he is utterly free to do things that we may or may not expect him to do; as the agent of his own freedom, that he exercises this freedom in the world as resurrected and so living; and that he will be seen most authentically for who he is when his actions surprise us. When the Father raised him from the grave, Jesus' life was certainly in many ways unprecedented and glorious, but it was also the very same life that he had been living all along. It is the life of obedience and radical outspokenness that got him into hot water with religious and political authorities and that ultimately led him to the cross. The continuities were obvious: he bore the scars for the original disciples to see; he *still* has the scars to this day; and, in their sacramental worship of him, Christians continue to tear the flesh that was torn, although their tearing is not really new tearing at all but a way of reenacting that single great event so long ago. Because Jesus is still living, though, our tearing and consuming includes us in that life that is now bigger than the life of an individual—it is, mysteriously of course, really the life of the church itself.

Nevertheless, this already edges its way slightly into the second, less straightforward sense of *unexpected* by which I mean to counsel an agenda for Christians—that we must learn to "un-expect" Jesus. Far from overidentifying Jesus with the church (as if the church were, against all appearances to the contrary, actually perfect and holy!), it is actually very important to think about how the church shares in the life of its living

---

10. Cited in von Balthasar, *Dare We Hope "That All Men Be Saved"?*, 161.

Unexpected Jesus

Lord without exhausting that life. When I talk about "un-expecting" Jesus, I have in mind this very dynamic: that confessing and coming to live with the fact that there is "more" to life than we can ever see or understand is actually, for the Christian, more a matter of confessing and coming to terms with the resurrection of Jesus than it is anything to do with life simply as such. So the agenda for the Christian in un-expecting Jesus is a way of engaging with life itself as first and foremost something whose mysteries are no more or less great than the mysteries Christians discover in a messiah who was once dead and is now living. How do we live with that?

We must free him from our controlling grasp, allow him to be the risen Christ, to stand over against the church as lord, judge, and servant whose agency neither evinces patterns of movement that are foregone conclusions nor displays a version of the good news that is easily packaged as "over and done with."[11] I am always especially eager to listen to Christmas and Easter sermons. I like to use the time of waiting that leads up to these great Holy Days to anticipate hearing and speaking things that we all, in a sense, already know, but in our knowing them also find ourselves confessing an openness to expecting greater or new insights each time around.

Like Lent, Advent also trains us to look and wait and hope. What are we waiting for? Do we simply and blissfully put out of our minds for a season the reality that we all know is right around the corner? Are we supposed to feign excitement and surprise when the star appears? No Christian ought to be satisfied with this. Surely the reason is that we *really are* still looking and waiting and hoping for something—Christ's glorious return, his setting right of all things according to his justice and mercy, his gathering of the nations to himself, and his establishment of right and blessed rule against tyranny, sorrow, loss, and suffering. This is the Christian hope, and Advent is the season in which we can most obviously practice it. But how do we practice something so grand and unusual? The key responsibility of Christians, if they are to be an Advent people, is to wait with purpose, to wait with *intent*. Un-expecting Jesus is a program for the church's divestment, a call for it to yield up and hand over its clutched-at securities and allow them to be converted to a trust that can never be more certain than the faithfulness of the one in whom it is placed.

---

11. See John Milbank's use of this phrase in *Theology and Social Theory*, 386–87.

Waiting with Intent

Once one begins looking, one notices this theme in a lot of places. It is a striking and very common motif in the New Testament: of watching for the coming of the Lord, of staying awake and not growing weary, of remaining vigilant and not losing heart. A sure sign that a people have given up waiting is their deep compromise with the world, especially with its timing. In *Waiting for Godot*, Samuel Beckett portrays those in the midst of waiting as caught in a mode of living in which the wait is so acute and overwrought that any meaning of life is perpetually deferred, indefinitely postponed. Life is the absence of meaning so long as the waiting it involves only suspends what it anticipates. We can certainly get so used to anything, even waiting for something else, that what used to feel like an activity with which we fill our time now becomes the very definition of time itself. We might even fail to recognize the passage of time if it were absent. To wait, in other words, may say nothing about the level of our hope and expectation that anything is going to happen. Disciples fervently await not only something that seems incredibly remote and outrageously improbable, but something that, against the odds, is really as certain as it is mysterious.

To lose hope is therefore exactly the same thing as to lose faith. When this happens, we cease structuring our lives around the cadence of the Christian life with God—liturgy and ecclesiastical cycles with special feast days and occasions to remember the saints and martyrs. We will instead start to find greater significance in national holidays, the natural seasons, and the academic calendar. Yet in this, we will not really be finding "significance" but only give ourselves to the numbing boredom of modern existence that substitutes cheap exchanges for meaningful remembrance. The surest sign of this is our identity as consumers and its primary function in structuring the calendar and in keeping in operation the national and global economies. Our waiting will have shifted from whatever the New Testament means by it to the anxiety that fills the time between now and the next purchase, a waiting that hardly deserves to be called waiting since every modern technological efficiency is clearly designed so that I no longer should have to wait for anything. Any delay that remains, therefore, is a problem to be solved by a further innovation.

Unexpected Jesus

In addition to the challenges that modern Christians clearly face if they are to be the kinds of waiters the New Testament envisions, there is also a perplexing theological question to consider. It has to do with the long-standing tradition within Christian thought called *negative* or *apophatic theology*. Negative theology is one way of preventing us from speaking nonsense when we talk about God. Our talking can only make use of the words we know how to use, and our use of them is conditioned by our familiarity with things in the world. The trouble, though, is that we are not familiar with God, and any attempt to describe what God is like, for example, will therefore surely be just as false as it is true, just as suggestive as it is misleading. There is a good deal of theology behind statements like this, and Thomas Aquinas is one of the major voices. For example, Thomas taught: "This is the ultimate in human knowledge of God: to know that we do not know him."[12]

Centuries earlier, Christianity faced a challenge by Islam to defend its use of images in worship. The prohibition against images of the divine is part of Christianity's Jewish identity and inheritance. The image always tempts us away from the thing it is pointing to and representing. It easily converts into an idol. And the problem with idols is the same problem with our words: they limit what they point to. They threaten precisely to circumscribe the object apart from the object doing so itself.[13] They can lead us to think that what they exhibit tells us without remainder what it is, what it is like, what its relation to us is like. So the prohibition against images is a safeguard against idolatry that shares the same impulse and logic as the later way of developing an appropriate mode of making claims about God using language. However, John of Damascus, the theologian who famously defended the use of images in Christian worship, made a strong (and for most of Christendom, convincing) christological argument for icons. Icons, John claimed, need not be idolatrous images because of Christ—the word has become flesh in Jesus; the unspeakable

---

12. Aquinas, *Disputed Questions on the Power of God*, 7.5. Ad 4; cited in Placher, *History of Christian Theology*, 154–55.

13. Since, for example, an entailment and expression of God's freedom is to, in a sense, circumscribe himself by being who he is as Father, Son, and Holy Spirit from all eternity. Circumscription as such is not a problem, though there is a difference between God *being* Trinity and our awareness of what is entailed in our confessing that he is. I am grateful to Jason Fout for helping clarify this distinction.

God has been spoken; the unseen God has been seen. And "we have beheld his glory" (John 1:14).

A classical negative theology is conscious of always being *nothing more than* a corrective element in our speech. By definition, its very existence depends on the negation of the affirmative and positive aspects of speaking, those things that attest to and are predicated of God as being true. It is only in a much more recent iteration that owes a great deal to the Continental philosophies of difference, otherness, and alterity that negative theology has slipped into purely negative affirmations. While these appear to exhibit their own dialectic ("negative affirmations" after all), they differ from their classical antecedents in belonging first to the discourse of absences. Oliver Davies and Denys Turner argue as much:

> Contemporary appropriations of negative theology, for all their validity, tend to set Christian negation apart from its affirmations, thus changing it from a negation of experience within a [classical] Dionysian dialectic to an experience of negation as such which has cut free from the liturgical and ecclesiastical contexts that originally supported it. This is to risk trading a mechanism of correction which maintains the truly theological and transcendental character of Christian affirmations for an ineffable "experience" which seems to validate the individual in his or her sublime independence of communal structures and commitments.[14]

Davies and Turner are right to caution us in this way. Negation on its own was never the point of doing negative theology in its original ways. It meant to discipline and round out the affirmations we make of God in order to make sure that, on occasion, we are actually able to move beyond modes of speaking that are designed to declare what God is like. Prayer is one such other mode.[15]

---

14. Davies and Turner, eds., *Silence and the Word*, 3–4.

15. For a discussion of this point, as well as a refutation of some contemporary philosophy, such as Derrida's, that insists on a stronger form of negation, see Marion, *In Excess*, ch. 6. Marion summarizes the way that Derrida suspects prayers that praise of smuggling in their own affirmations (since God is praised for being *this way*) and thus being different from prayers plain and simple (134). The tradition of negative theology has not always thought this to be an objection. As I explain in chapter 3 of the present volume, the creeds are themselves prayers (ending with *Amen*) for the faith to believe what we are confessing. Like prayers of praise, creeds show that it is possible for our speech to affirm some things, predicating them of God, without being exclusively affirmative and predicative.

Theologically, the Christian church has long emphasized that God's unknowability has little to do with ideas about God's ultimate vagueness or the mysteriousness of what remains ill-defined. The problem does not have to do with a God who refuses to speak, who is determined to remain hidden and unseen, or who, in speaking, refuses to give us the true divine self. Rather, in affirming the Son of God as God's own Word-utterance, not only *from* himself but *as* himself, Christianity is not preserving for God some unuttered aspects of the divine self that render partial our speaking of him. Our speaking *is* partial, incomplete, and never definitive (short of glory, and perhaps not even then). But these are not the reasons. The reason is that the manner in which God has definitively revealed himself is in a *life*—the kind of thing that is known through relationship, that makes room for others to come into God's embrace, and not as static knowledge. Jesus Christ reveals God as a life and issues the invitation to know God accordingly. Herein lies the problem for how we speak about God: not that God has given himself too little but too much; the giving is as present as it is past, particularly if how God gave Jesus—in the past in resurrection—is definitive and true. "His everlasting act is as little capable of being a determinate object to our minds as the wind in our faces and lungs can be held still and distant in front of our eyes."[16] What we know of God is not too little to speak of properly; it is too much. In making this christological move, the tradition preserves the identity of God's nature with God's will and action. God cannot be known as passive, though not because the human mind is limited; the reason is that there is no nature of God that is passive with respect to the Son. We are involved in, and part of, God's act. We are not mere observers of it.

There is another way that classical negative theology is at variance with contemporary philosophical trends that, in part, nevertheless still resemble it. As Davies and Turner suggest, Christian negative theology does not countenance the independence from tradition that these trends claim for themselves. The pressure of postmodern anxieties concerning making any affirmations at all often arises from an all too modern longing for detachment. Disengaged from reasoning communities (in the present case, ecclesial ones) that make possible affirming one thing as opposed to another, the postmodern self must maintain suspicion of its own communication, lest it be found holding commitments for which it can give

---

16. Williams, *Arius*, 242.

no justifiable account. The Christian knowledge of God, however, always first takes the form of gospel in which the community that proclaims this news cannot be ancillary to the proclamation it makes. The Christian self is brought into and is produced by the church, a community that Robert Jenson describes as "a visible and very ordinary assembly of persons, when what has assembled them is the communicating of the gospel."[17] The church does not preexist this communicating; the communicating, in fact, constitutes it. Nor do those assembled as church exist by a prior communication that is now over and done with, something spoken by others in the past that now carries no burden to speak in the present what can only be possible for a people who believe their common life to owe to the continual work of God. The abundance of God's disclosure, even to the point of incarnating a new people who bear the promise of an entire new creation, is consistent with this.

The idea of promise reemerges again at precisely this point. A people who speak the gospel as truth include themselves as part of the goodness the gospel proclaims. Nevertheless, because the gospel is still "other" to the church (at least in the sense that the church does not simply proclaim itself), the church heralds a goodness that it does not create, just as it testifies to its own existence as God's work. The ways that Christians still find to speak the gospel will of necessity be various. "Precisely to be itself, the gospel is never told the same way twice."[18] The continuity of God's people who tell the gospel over time—across the centuries and indeed across the globe—therefore depends on the truth of the gospel, which is to say the manner and specificity of what it claims to be true: that Jesus Christ lives a risen life and so exists contemporaneously with the church in its catholicity. The church's boldness in its innovative speaking of the gospel will be a function of its determination to remain faithful to its own history. Even so, this stability cannot be bought by sacrificing the innovation of the gospel proclamation and clinging to a frozen past without also undoing the promise that the gospel is. Promise unites the church across time *because* Jesus Christ is alive in history. These are not two promises—two gospels—but one and the same gospel and promise.

We are left with some questions coming out of this brief interchange between John's defense of images and the *via negativa*: Is there a danger

17. Jenson, *Story and Promise*, 2.
18. Ibid., 11.

in over-knowing Jesus? Can we make the mistake of rendering him "over-revealed"? Is there, in other words, something in this dialectic that can serve today's church in its attempts to know Jesus without over-knowing him? I do not only intend this to be a theoretical question about the nature of God or the identity of Jesus Christ. Put crudely but not inaccurately, one worry might be that in a Christian zeal to "know Christ," we unwittingly but dangerously only know him as a version of ourselves, a version of the cultural world we inhabit, and a participant within the systems of exchange and power that we take for granted.

chapter two

Staying Awake

"Blessed are those servants whom the master finds awake when he comes... You also must be ready; for the Son of man is coming at an unexpected hour." (Luke 12:37, 40)

The Christian gospel is nothing if it is not good news for strangers. Even though strangers will explicitly be the topic of a later chapter, they also, in a sense, animate this whole book. If Jesus is really to be *un-expected*, he will in the process become to us more strange, though not less of a friend. This chapter is therefore both about strangers becoming friends and friends becoming strange. The discussion unfolds through a consideration of what it means for Christians to be a people awake.

Two of Christianity's greatest modern strangers enrich our thinking about sleep and wakefulness: Albert Camus and Friedrich Nietzsche. In his monumental diagnosis of the modern self, *The Stranger*, Camus presents a central character who frequently and lazily gives himself to sleep. Is it out of boredom? Perhaps Meursault sees no real difference between being awake and sleeping. Does he even, we may wonder, acknowledge *any* qualitative differences between anything? His is an existence marked by indifference. Yet in the final chapter, he stays awake in order *not to be surprised* by the coming judgment and justice he must face: the execution of his death sentence. Confronted with an impending future, he no longer can abide in the blithe serenity of a life judged equivalent with death, wakefulness equivalent to sleep. He does not want to be caught with his guard down since only in being awake can he resolutely stand against the intentions of others.

Similarly, in *Thus Spoke Zarathustra*, Nietzsche presents the "last man" as the embodiment of a culture that loves sleep. It prefers the fantasies that dreams readily serve up; it more readily believes them and finds them to be true. Yet it is not exactly a culture indifferent to truth; it merely willingly submits to the self-deception that turns dreams into the new reality. It *prefers* the version of reality that fantasy provides. The will to truth puts up no fight against this and so the fantasies face no resistance. More fundamental than the ideas of truth and reality, then, are the strength or weakness of a people's will to confront them for what they are. This is signaled by their determination to remain awake.

We might call this kind of wakefulness the tenacious acceptance of reality's most honest mode of being. Rather than fancifully inhabiting a dream world, the human awake desires no other world if it means not also having this one. Nietzsche reflected on whether we would consider our dreams more "real" than the real world if the same dream continued night after night and if we were more successful in them than in our real lives. If the dream were continuous and, like our "real life," picked up right where it left off, or even (more like our "real life") continued through our waking hours only to have us rejoin it when we sleep again, we might begin to switch them in our minds. We might start to mistake wakefulness for sleep and vice versa.[1] Nietzsche was convinced that our biological need for rest is easily subordinated to our wills to believe the reality of one life over another. In fact, the strongest part of Nietzsche's observation in this regard is the implication that all of us already do this anyway. He can be cavalier about notions like "real life" for exactly this reason. Regardless of whether or not they appear in a dream or are real (*really* real, that is), we will nevertheless always think of our deepest fantasies as reality so long as we allow ourselves to do so.[2]

Our ability to stay awake depends on our will to face the truth—about ourselves and about all reality—even when it is painful. Will we live in ways that press us ever deeper into being truthful about what is

---

1. See Nietzsche, *Birth of Tragedy*, sec. 1, and "On Truth and Lies in a Nonmoral Sense," 87.

2. If this is true, then "really real" does not help to clarify anything at all.

Staying Awake

real and that require us to confront the roughness of the road we walk? Wakefulness means not closing our eyes to what is happening around us. It prefers the unvarnished brutality of the actual world to a dreamlike world of easily recognized types. It knows it is more difficult to look than to imagine and that doing so demands great labor and effort. Wakeful eyes are not easily coaxed to close themselves.

It is true that Christians have too often represented the opposite: a fanciful view of *true* reality that countenances disdain for the world as it appears. It has done this not only on account of the redemption that all of creation awaits, but somehow as marked by what can only be called a counter-redemption. It refuses to find good in God's good creation and prefers a reality so utterly different from this world that one wonders whether, in its scorn, it has handed human history over to a fate that can only with difficulty find God's presence within it at all. This posture toward the world condemns more wholeheartedly than does God, seeks a salvation of the world (notably *from* the world) that leaves the world behind, and escapes from the weightier matters of incarnation, love, and devotion in favor of every kind of distance.

Nietzsche made no effort to hide his deep antipathy for Raphael's painting of Jesus's transfiguration for this exact reason. Looking at the exalted Christ distracts us from what is real—it makes unthinkable every misery and loathsome human suffering. It diverts our gaze from what is earthward and terrestrial in every other way and tempts us to look up.

> Raphael, himself one of those immortal "naïve" artists, in a symbolic canvas has illustrated that reduction of illusion to further illusion.... In the lower half of his "Transfiguration," through the figures of the possessed boy, the despairing bearers, the helpless, terrified disciples, we see the reflection of original pain, the sole ground of being: "illusion" here is a reflection of eternal contradiction, begetter of all things. From this illusion there rises, like the fragrance of ambrosia, a new illusory world, invisible to those enmeshed in the first: a radiant vision of pure delight, a rapt seeing through wide-open eyes.[3]

The suffering of the possessed boy, as well as the confusion and desperation of the onlookers, while real, is something away from which Raphael encourages readers to look. Instead, he presents to the viewer something much more compelling and beautiful even while it is, in Nietzsche's

---

3. Nietzsche, *Birth of Tragedy*, sec. 4.

estimation, pure fantasy. Gazing upward to Christ and away from the pain of life is not only one of the main functions of religion; it also betrays a fundamental dissatisfaction with life as it actually is. Presented with a greater ideal as an invention of the yearning we feel for the world to be something other than how we find it to be, we will forsake what is real and ultimately hate life itself, spurred on by the hope that it be transformed into something that it is not. Nietzsche set himself the task of the opposite, affirming life in all of its wretchedness.[4]

Indeed, in his commentary on St. Matthew's Gospel, the third-century theologian Origen interprets the transfiguration scene in ways that Nietzsche would have despised, had he read it.

> If therefore any one of us wishes to be taken by Jesus, and led up by Him into the high mountain, and be deemed worthy of beholding His transfiguration apart, let him pass beyond the six days, because he no longer beholds the things which are seen, nor longer loves the world, nor the things in the world (1 John 2.15) nor lusts after any worldly lust, which is the lust of bodies, and of the riches of the body, and of the glory which is after the flesh, and whatever things whose nature it is to distract and drag away the soul from the things which are better and diviner, and bring it down and fix it fast to the deceit of this age, in wealth and glory, and the rest of the lusts which are the foes of truth. For when he has passed through the six days, as we have said, he will keep a new Sabbath, rejoicing in the lofty mountain, because he sees Jesus transfigured before him; for the Word has different forms, as He appears to each as is expedient for the beholder, and is manifested to no one beyond the capacity of the beholder.[5]

Origen clearly thought that what is true and real is Christ in his glory and the scene's ability to rescue us from being distracted by what is passing away. One of the interesting questions here is about what the transfiguration of Christ is showing us, what it is prefiguring. There are clear elements that seem to imply that it has something to do with Christ's return in glory since it is a revelation of the Son's dramatic glorification,

---

4. In *The Question of Ethics*, Charles Scott describes well Nietzsche's way of affirming life as it is: "This affirmation does not promise an end to butchery and chaotic insensitivity, but it does provide an awareness of misery, a region for the fullness of its sounds, that is not to be escaped by ideals, goals, and visions that often define our subjection to what we must consider to be the best way of life" (174).

5. Origen, *Commentary on Matthew*, 12.36 (Patrick, 469).

Staying Awake

complete with the co-reign or co-glorification of the living-though-dead saints, Moses and Elijah. Moreover, the episode is preceded with Jesus declaring, "Truly, I say to you, there are some standing here who will not taste death before they see the Son of man coming in his kingdom" (Matt 16:28). Yet many have supposed Christ's transfiguration to prefigure his resurrection. I will not argue the point at length here, but I think this is mistaken. I am instead persuaded that it prefigures the cross. How so?

The transfiguration is an event that at some level is meant for the disciples' benefit. Yet their confusion and lack of faith about what Jesus had been foretelling did not arise from their inability to understand his claim about rising again three days after being killed (Mark 8:31). What they refused to countenance is that this Jesus whom they (Peter at least) had come to believe to be God's Messiah would suffer, would be rejected and killed. When the voice of God speaks, the message is a simple one: listen to Jesus (Mark 9:7). The disciples are being indicted for their refusal to listen to the hard news that Jesus had been sharing with them just prior to this. A suffering Messiah did not comport with their ideas about what is supposed to happen to the Messiah. The philosopher Merold Westphal helpfully glosses Peter's objection—"God forbid it, Lord! This must never happen to you" (Matt 16:22). He interprets Peter to be saying: "This does not fall within the conditions of possible experience . . . . Such a Messiah does not, yea, cannot occur within our horizons of expectation. We have no noetic acts at our disposal to constitute you as crucified criminal."[6] The disciples must be met with an event surprising enough to break them out of their preconceived notions of a messiah's role and mission—their ideas of glory, power, and even salvation.

When Jesus speaks about the cross, he is not heard, so the glorified manner in which he is transfigured before the disciples is accompanied by a voice that confirms that the offense of the cross is real. Westphal explains that the challenge to Peter, James, and John partly refuses to dissociate the offense and scandal of the cross from Jesus. The challenge asks, "Do you have the faith to believe *still* that *this* Jesus, who overwhelms all your horizons of expectations . . . is the Christ, the Son of the living God?"[7] The transfiguration *is* a glorious vision and presence but decidedly *not* of the sort that the disciples expected for the Messiah. It is as if the event occurs

---

6. Westphal, "Transfiguration as Saturated Phenomenon," 31. I am indebted to Westphal's interpretation of the transfiguration in several respects.

7. Ibid., 32.

in order to say that if you fail to see the glory in the cross, you will just as surely fail to notice Christ's resurrection and the return.

Now, where does this leave Raphael and Nietzsche's critique? Can Raphael be redeemed? Can we long for glory, completion, deliverance, and holiness without being distracted from hurt, confusion, and suffering? Does Christian belief, at its heart, accord with the words of the French Surrealist poet Paul Éluard, who remarked, "There is another world, but it is in this one"? Is it possible to look on Jesus with eyes that are open to everything else in the world, eyes that are even *more open* to the world because they are also fixed on Jesus?

I think so, but it will call for a great deal of wakefulness—the kind that, through discipline, comes to recognize Christ's exaltation in unexpected places. The Orthodox theologian Alexander Schmemann reflects on how epiphanies always have a sacramental character—they reveal to us the true meaning of something by showing us what it is like for the thing to be most fully itself. In the light of God, things are often seen to be *more complex* than in other lights. Schmemann argues against the religious tendency that Nietzsche also identified, namely, to separate absolutely what is sacred from what is profane. It is nearly a firm, horizontal line in Raphael's painting, separating heavenly from earthly.

A robust understanding of the sacraments renders dichotomies such as these problematic. Schmemann gives the example of holy water and two possible ways of thinking about it. One is to ponder that something mundane and profane has been transformed into something religious and sacred. This thought emphasizes that what was once "merely" water is now quite unlike water for having been taken up into God's use of it. Schmemann objects to this for reasons that Nietzsche would have appreciated: when something is considered religious, it is lifted out of the ordinary life of things. "Here the act of blessing reveals nothing about water, and thus about matter or world."[8] Rather, what is sacred is sacred because it is no longer what it was or even what it usually is—profane. But there is another way to think about such things. "The same act of blessing," continues Schmemann, "may mean the revelation of the true 'nature' and 'destiny' of water, and thus of the world." The blessing of the water, its being made part of the sacrament it undergoes, actually restores and reveals water's true function and its reason for being water in the first place.

---

8. Schmemann, *For the Life of the World*, 132.

In the same way, all of creation is shown to have sacramental potential, *not* for being capable of being rescued from its true self, but exactly the opposite—all of creation is able to be used by a God who *through such use* discloses its true meaning.⁹

Most Christians will be able to recognize that a well-intentioned religiosity and piety may actually fall prey to refusing much continuity between religion and the rest of life. Schmemann makes the point that this very piety is paradoxically shared by the most fervent secularist. "Having nothing to reveal about world and matter, about time and nature, this idea and this experience of worship 'disturb' nothing, question nothing, challenge nothing, are indeed 'applicable' to nothing. They can therefore peacefully 'coexist' with any secular ideology, and form of secularism."¹⁰

This is what is more typical of Christianity in the West today. It is the reason that Nietzsche's critique of Raphael has merit no matter how the transfiguration is understood. We might call it Christianity asleep. It is an active preference to be numbed by dreams of the next life while becoming remote from and passive to this one. This kind of sleep also identifies an ecclesiological shortcoming. Or perhaps it just reveals the lack of good faith. Christians asleep have no need for the church, preferring the arrival of future realities in all their clarity to gifts that are much more difficult to discern in the present. This sleep longs for a church that does not now exist: purified and much more faithful, better able to face God. But when the sleeper does this, he neglects the church that is even now on its way to God, the generations who, in their current struggle with divided loyalties and pale hopes, nevertheless walk to God according to his promises. The modern dysfunction of solitary Christianity, however, only self-righteously transfers the burden of faithfulness from the church to the individual. It imagines the full range of God's gifts to be at the ready service of every Christian, weighing down the individual body with a mission that was only ever meant for the collective one. Such a sleeper slumbers in failure to see both God's activity, in spite of everything, in

---

9. Catherine Pickstock makes the same point about the whole liturgy: "[W]ithin the logic of Catholic liturgy, if one goes to the altar, which prefigures the altar set in the middle of the heavenly Jerusalem, then one does so as *oneself*. In fact, one *only becomes oneself* in doing so" (Pickstock, "Liturgy and Modernity," 25, emphasis original). In the same way, in baptism, "the person is irrevocably changed, but only to what one already was. It makes the person *more* himself, rather than setting a barrier between the previously impure self and the new initiated self" (34).

10. Schmemann, *For the Life of the World*, 133.

the broken vessels of present churchly existence and also the brokenness of the sleeping self, even more hopeless without the church than with it. The church, in other words, has understandably invited a debate about its visibility and invisibility, even while substituting the more evidently transparent self hardly settles it.[11]

There are other forms of neglect. For example, Gregory of Nyssa points to a kind of preoccupation with the life of this world that is distorted for failing to recognize God as the source and end of all things. "The Lord has given His disciples many precepts by which their minds might shake off all material elements, like so much clay, and thus rise to a desire for the Transcendent. And one of these is that all who are seriously concerned with the life of heaven must conquer sleep . . . ."[12] And who are the sleepers?

> By drowsiness and sleep here I am referring to those dreamlike fantasies which are shaped by those who are submerged in the deceptions of this life: I mean public office, money, influence, external show, the seduction of pleasure, love of reputation and enjoyment, honor, and all the other worldly things which, by some sort of illusion, are sought after vainly by those who live without reflection. For all these things will pass away with the flux of time; their existence is mere seeming; they are not what we think they are . . .[13]

According to Gregory, we are not tempted and lulled to sleep by visions of another, better world than the one God created. We are instead seduced by a vision of that creation as separated from God. The vanities he enumerates are neither natural nor suited to the goodness of what God has made—they are, in this sense, false and illusory. What is real is life with God in God's world.

For the Gospels, the charge to remain awake (for example, in the parable of the wedding party and in the garden of Gethsemane) conveys more than the admonition to "be vigilant." It says also and perhaps much more importantly, "Do not fear the truth. Only then will you see Jesus." A fear of truth is more fundamental than not knowing it since our fearless

---

11. It scarcely needs mentioning that the concept of the "invisible church" is always an indictment against the "visible church," and the distinction is surely something that could only be invented by those who hold to the fallibility of Christians while yet holding onto a perfect ideal.

12. Gregory of Nyssa, *Homilies on the Song of Songs*, in *From Glory to Glory*, 243.

13. Ibid.

seeking after it meets God's promise that we will find it. Overcoming fear of the truth therefore begins with boldly admitting that we do not know what we will find, what the truth will turn out to be, and how displeasing we may find it. In one of Jesus' parables, all of the bridesmaids fall asleep when they were made to wait longer than expected for the bridegroom (Matthew 25). At midnight, an hour when one presumably expects the arrival of no one, there is a shout: "Look! Here is the bridegroom! Come out to meet him" (v. 6). Whereupon five of the ten bridesmaids, having had the foresight to bring along enough oil, come forth with their lamps. The others, for lack of oil, watch their lamps grow dim and, when they go to buy more, miss the bridegroom's arrival and are shut out of the wedding banquet (v. 10). Stanley Hauerwas comments on this parable: "The foolish bridesmaids failed to understand that in a time when you are unsure of the time you are in it is all the more important to do what you have been taught to do. In the dark you must keep the lamps ready if they are not able to overcome the darkness."[14] The bridegroom comes to discover that some, and not others, have been waiting with patience by doing the work that Jesus has given them to do.

Augustine understood this indisputably to be a story about judgment. On his reading, the time of waiting is also the time of mercy—God's mercy *is itself* the time given to wait for the consummation of all things in which God's people will enjoy the heavenly banquet as his guests.[15] God gives his mercy to creatures by prolonging the time before they must face judgment. Within this time, the church lives and extends its mission to the nations with the good news that the God who judges is also the same God who shows mercy, indeed has already shown mercy by being to the world the merciful Son. This one's gift to the world of himself is also the time given for his exercise of mercy toward those who deserve judgment.[16] Even so, this mercy-time is still a period of anticipation, for

14. Hauerwas, *Matthew*, 209.

15. Augustine, *Sermon 23*, par. 16 (MacMullen, 405).

16. In a parallel manner, Karl Barth saw that God's mercy also collapses with God's righteousness where both intersect with his special concern for the poor and vulnerable: "God's righteousness does not really stand alongside His mercy, but . . . according to Scripture, with the plight of the poor and wretched, it is itself God's mercy. Just because He is righteous God has mercy, condescending sympathetically to succor those who are utterly in need of His help, who without it would in fact be lost" (Barth, *Church Dogmatics*, II.1, 387). Like Barth's, the effort here is toward giving a nonformal account of mercy. I undertake a nonformal account of forgiveness in chapter 5 below.

the time of the bridegroom's arrival marks the end of the time of mercy and the beginning of the time of judgment.

Moreover, God is Lord of both judgment and mercy. Jürgen Moltmann teaches that the gospel elicits a human expectation that is not finally at odds with divine judgment:

> Even the coming judgment of the living and the dead is a subject for *hope*, for longing and the prayer, "Come soon, Lord Jesus!" For who is the judge? It is the same Christ who gave himself up to death for sinners and who has borne our griefs and sicknesses. How should we not trust ourselves joyfully to this judgment? What will the crucified Jesus judge us by? The law, or his own gospel? Our own acts, or his sufferings for us? How should we not hasten joyfully to meet the universal judge when he is the one who was crucified for us? And finally—what will be the purpose of his judgment? The punishment of the wicked and the reward of the good? Or will his intention be to establish his righteousness everywhere and in everyone? Will he judge us in order to annihilate us, or to save us—to cast us down, or to raise us up? Does the Last Judgment know any other kind of divine righteousness and justice than what we experience here and now in the justification of sinners? . . . It is only when it is based on the remembrance and present experience of Christ that judgment points in the direction of *his* future. His righteousness will triumph! He, the crucified Jesus, will judge! He will judge according to his gospel![17]

Those who stay awake await with eager anticipation the arrival of the bridegroom. They are prepared to celebrate with him no matter the hour. The Judge who comes is none other than the wounded and victorious Jesus of Nazareth, who already came at Bethlehem and has refused to abandon us to our abandonment of him. The coming judgment is not an end of the good news, but an extension of it. Still, the message here is not only one about keeping awake, but of being ready even in sleep: "But if we are all to sleep, how shall we watch? Watch with the heart, watch with faith, watch with hope, watch with charity, watch with good works."[18] Crucially for the story, all of the bridesmaids are subject to and receive judgment. It is a mistake so to separate mercy and judgment that we imagine that God's exercise of mercy is not simultaneously an act of judgment and also the reverse: that God's exercise of judgment is also an act of mercy. The

17. Moltmann, *Experiences of God*, 35.
18. Augustine, *Sermon* 43, par. 17 (MacMullen, 405).

Staying Awake

difference between the two groups of bridesmaids, then, is in their *preparation* for being unexpected by the bridegroom's coming. Awake lamps, properly fueled, signal the church's willingness to acknowledge God's acts at odd times (midnight), to see them as God's authentic works among us, to undergo the discipline necessary to see them this way. They signal that the church is at ease with a wild God whose surprise appearances are not so ultimately shocking that the church denies God's freedom so to act, or at least must choose between denying God this freedom or ceasing to be the church altogether.

It is perhaps one of the great ironies that parables like this one have so easily in Christian history been enlisted in projects for detailing the certainty of the salvation of some and the damnation of others. Some have been tempted to name the bridesmaids, with their own names given to the faithful and their enemies' names given to the unfaithful. But does this kind of certainty not cut against the very grain of the parable's teaching? Later in the same chapter, the sheep are separated from the goats—the righteous from the unrighteous—in a similar fashion that the bridesmaids were separated (Matt 25:31–46; see chapter 7 in this book). Crucially, *both* groups were surprised by the judgment. It was unexpected—neither group presumed that they had been either aiding or neglecting Jesus in their aid or neglect of the "least of these." The difference is in the waiting-activity, which, as Augustine says, is a watching with the heart. But it is likely that a vastly different kind of waiting and watching is produced by knowing ahead of time how the outcome of the judgment will transpire, who is included and who is not. In this case, the only thing that is certain is the judgment, which then ought properly to inspire the necessary preparation without spoiling the surprise. After all, many will presumably enter into glory with knowledge of these parables, but others may not. Knowing more than that quite simply threatens to make them untrue.

This last comment raises the question: Why then do we even have this parable? Does it not threaten to ruin the surprise or to somehow corrupt our waiting? It seems to me that the only answer can be that it intends to uncouple our knowing and our certainty from our acts of mercy. These acts of generosity and compassion are disabled from being tied to a motivation for reward. Readers of these parables are, on the one hand, given insight into Jesus Christ's character as definitive for every eschatological reckoning, ensuring that the compassionate Galilean is identical with the triumphant Son of Man, that the man of sorrows delights in his victory, that the lamb is the same as the conquering lion. Yet this is a knowledge that—if it translates into anything at all—clearly translates more into works of mercy than it does into the certainty of a favorable judgment on the basis of the knowledge itself. This is signaled supremely by the fact that the news given to both groups comes as a surprise to them.

Recall the kind of wakefulness of which Camus reminds us—one that is surely less salutary and more subtly insidious. Not the hopeful anticipation of what is to come, but a bleary, bloodshot restlessness. The sleep-deprived are tormented by their wakefulness: they fear the present reality but fear the alternatives even more. It is a wakefulness that is no longer allowed to be bored as before, no longer permitted to rest indifferent to life or death, love or rage, waking or sleeping. Nevertheless, Meursault is a vigilant man. In a Gospel idiom, again, we would say that he lives by fear rather than by faith; his suffering is impending dread and ironically, perhaps, more known than a hope that lives by promise. He believes in foregone conclusions, is mindful of how fate conspires against him, and even though up until now he always viewed stories like this from the outside, his living it now brings its utter predictability crashing down on him.

Against this, Christian watchfulness is a profound disbelief in the impersonal power of fate. The universe, for the Christian, does not unwind according to a preset course of events. Nor does it evince the rigid laws of cause and effect that would generate a precise ethic along the lines of a karma-style justice that is based on the exact and careful repayment of good for good and evil for evil. Rather, God's justice has to do with the cross, beyond every calculation and predictability. No one will recognize Jesus by directly watching for him. We would, after all, have to know what to look for in order for this to work. Instead, there is a more fundamental move for recognizing him—by welcoming the disclosure of all truth. The New Testament suggests this in speaking of dwelling "in the light" (e.g., John 12:36), not fearing the darkness. If there is a commendable Advent wakefulness, a noble way of resisting the temptation toward business as usual while we expect something we have not yet known, then it involves our openness to the free movements of Christ in the world even as we now know it.

Rather than imagining that what Christians await will be readily seen by everyone when it comes, let us instead imagine that seeing it demands a certain kind of vision. It is "he who does the will of [Jesus'] Father" (Matt 7:21) and the pure in heart who are promised to "see God" (Matt 5:8). The church season of Advent appropriately intermingles Christ's first coming and his second coming, Bethlehem and the end of the age. I confess that I imagine Christ's return to be very much like his arrival the first time: unsuspecting, easy to miss. He will show up where many least expect him: in Tijuana or Mali, perhaps. In this respect, the church plays the role of the prophets and, most immediately, of John the Baptist. It teaches people how to look for and recognize Jesus against the background of the world that threatens to obscure him, a world that specializes in distracting us from the momentous event of the arrival of the Son of God, making him invisible—if not absolutely, then certainly very much in actual fact. The church, in its worship, its moral formation, and its catechesis, trains Christian sights on those things that easily pass us by unnoticed. This is the more obvious sense in which disciples must be awake—not poised to welcome a cataclysmic event that will make others cower, but sensitive to small movements and with an ear tuned to tiny voices.

The church is not, even now, without the resources to practice these things. When wealthy Christians set their influence to the service of the weak and poor, we should not primarily think of this as "charity" (in the modern, condescending sense) but as the responsiveness of riches to a love (*caritas*) seldom practiced and not easily justified among the rich.[19] Even so, it is still a way God has given his people for practicing an alertness to poverty and weakness that, in turn, displays an Advent wakefulness, turning a self-consumed attention toward others for the sake of a busyness in the work of the kingdom that cannot but notice the arrival of the ultimate stranger.

It is true that there is a great tradition that focuses on the dramatic aspects of Christ's arrival. Jesus quotes from Daniel's prophecy about the Son of Man "coming on the clouds of heaven with power and great glory"; the sun and moon will be darkened, the heavens will shake, and the elect will be gathered from the four winds (Matt 24:30–31). While these events would no doubt be difficult to miss, it is actually common to miss the ways that the New Testament very often actually would have us see them coming about through the event of the cross. For example, Matthew reports that Jesus' death was preceded by three hours of darkness while at

19. Catherine Pickstock points out that life was more "liturgical" in the High Middle Ages, an indication of which can be seen in the bonds that charity created and sustained. "Charity was seen as a holy event, a sacred state of being that had to involve a real exchange and intimacy between the participants. Here it was impossible for charity to be a remote and bureaucratic transaction" (Pickstock, "Liturgy and Modernity," 26).

the moment of his death, the earth shook, the rocks were split, and the tombs of the saints were opened (Matt 27:45, 51–53). While these are eschatological events, we are remiss if we only look on them as aspects of Christ's future life, of his return in glory. Perhaps we are being warned that seeing God's signs is more complex than we thought, that it is actually subtle and easily missed. If we neglect the ways that the cross is really an eschatological event of glory that darkens the sky and shakes the earth and heavens, what makes us think that all eyes will turn to see Christ in his promised, dramatic return? Could it be that looking for this is, in truth, a sure way to be robbed by a thief in the night?

Nevertheless, a danger lies in this way of thinking. It may lead us to separate the work of the kingdom that the church has now been called on to do from the future work of God. We know we are already tempted to separate our work from God's *present* activity, mistaking "our" work as completely our own, confused about where God "fits." The proper response to both of these—present and future—is to depend on a sufficiently sacramental understanding of human action. As creatures, nothing that we create is "out of nothing" as is God's creating. Ours is nevertheless tied into the creative work of God, mysteriously and with a certain amount of ambiguity as to where our creating ends and God's begins. It is also less linear than this: our actions are *within* God's actions, upheld and extended by divine creativity. This is most clearly the case with the sacraments.

Eucharist, for example, takes ordinary food and transforms it into nourishment for our spirits; the profane becomes holy. The precise nature of "transforms" and "becomes" has clearly been the subject of much theological debate. But it seems crucial that we need to be able to affirm both its staying the same and its changing, in some respect or another. Orthodoxy is notoriously difficult to pin down; heresies are usually much easier to identify. In this case, wrong teachings likely lie on both sides: one side affirming that nothing has changed whatsoever (a view usually associated with Zwingli, though in practice now extremely widespread among Protestants); the other side affirming that everything has changed (a view sometimes called "sensualist" that takes the change to be so complete that, with sufficient faith, the recipient will actually taste flesh and blood).

Both of these err. One errs by making ourselves into the exclusive agents of the "sacrament" (which cannot therefore properly be a sacrament). The other one errs by making God the exclusive agent. The truth lies somewhere in between. The sacraments are a microcosm of the larger church-event in the world, especially as it relates to the kingdom of God. Put differently, the church has neither *nothing* to do with the kingdom (one that remains wholly future to the church) nor *everything* to do with the kingdom. Precisely parsing the ways that the visible church does not coincide with the kingdom of God was a favorite Reformation theme. However, it is likely that there must remain an appropriate ambiguity to this question or else it will refute itself. There is more to the kingdom than the church; Christ is present in the world in more ways than Christians or anyone else can now conceive; the good news is present in places where it is still yet to be known; God is at work in enemies of the faith. The key to noticing all of this is a sacramental "more," a eucharistic excess.

The sacraments are some ways Christians have been given for staying awake. They function as part of what is anything but an idle waiting. They are rather part of an active patience in which the work of God's presence is enacted and discovered, narrated and welcomed. Nevertheless, to know it, to possess it, kills the "more" that Christians confess to find within the risen life of Jesus Christ. Christ's excess *is* his continuation of his risen life among us and for us, still in the world. How did he leave the world at the ascension? If the body of Christ was created as such at Pentecost as the creation of the church out of a collection of frightened disciples in an upper room, then his living Spirit brought him back, returned him to the world in their very presence as a grace-constituted community. Can Christians, then, learn to recognize Christ in—even *as*—the church, made present to it as already a kind of return, an early Advent?

Certain strands of Protestantism shrink from the *as* in the previous sentence (Christ *as* the church). They worry that claiming that the church is the body of Christ says too much, that it risks overidentifying the corporate existence Christians share with the one who ought more properly to stand over against that existence. Theology risks becoming excessively institutional. This worry has some merit. What is astute about it is its recognition that the church dare not suppose that its every act has God on its side and that the teaching authority of the church ought not to be collapsed completely with the authority of either Christ or Scripture.[20] Such concerns are also shared by some Catholics who see in Vatican II a real, though sometimes halfhearted, attempt to help the church avoid turning in on itself.[21]

---

20. Treier, *Virtue and the Voice of God*, ch. 3.
21. Gutiérrez, *Theology of Liberation*, esp. 258–62. Gutiérrez sees the appeal in some

Nevertheless, as William Cavanaugh argues, the alternative may be worse. The idea that Christ is wholly other to the church may actually become more attractive to the church in a self-fulfilling manner. Cavanaugh claims that "many contemporary Christians have shied away from the image of the church as the body of Christ, for naming the church as Christ's very body rings of the ecclesiastical triumphalism of the past . . . however, the unfaithfulness of the church in the present age is based to some extent precisely on its failure to take itself seriously as the continuation of Christ's body in the world and to conform itself, body and soul, not to the world but to Christ."[22] In other words, inscribing a distance between Christ and the church (that, in an extreme form, is clearly foreign to the New Testament, we should add) out of a desire to allow Christ to judge it may in practice function to give him more to judge. Some will argue that the excessive disunity and individualism of some forms of Protestantism ought not to be blamed on Reformers like Luther and Calvin but rather on a departure from their teaching.[23] But this has historically been more of a tendency in Protestant thought than in Catholic thought, and probably for reasons that, while complex, are not unconnected to a reticence to link Christ with his body, the church.

Even so, the church does not finally constrain the free Christ. The church's learning so to recognize Christ in and as the church *entirely depends* on its success in discovering him *outside* the church. This answers a characteristically Protestant worry of overidentifying Christ with the church, a concern that any critical distance in which Christ must continue to exercise his authority over the church will simply collapse into it. Robert Jenson asks how the church can be appropriately subordinated to Christ—the head of the church—if the church is simultaneously Christ's presence in the church. Are we inevitably led to a triumphalistic church?[24]

Jenson's own answer to this worry is to argue that the church is Christ's availability to me in that the unity of the assembly is constituted by the presence within it of something distinct from it—the Eucharist.[25]

---

of the Vatican II documents to understand the church as a sacrament as a positive step toward avoiding an "ecclesiocentric perspective" in which the church overidentifies its role in God's plan of salvation.

22. Cavanaugh, *Torture and Eucharist*, 233.
23. Treier argues this in *Virtue and the Voice of God*, esp. 87.
24. Jenson, "Church and Sacraments," 212.
25. Ibid., 210.

In its eucharistic activity the church engages in a complex relation with the gifting and the gift. The church gives itself to an identification with the presence of Christ through receiving the Eucharist in a way that simultaneously makes clear that Christ is given to the church as an availability that, by definition, comes from a source other than itself. Christ's givenness to the believer through and as the community of faith is precisely the means by which the believer is made a member of it.

In this way, the church may grow used to recognizing what is good for itself from outside of itself. The main constituting rite of the church's existence is a training ground for its faculties of perception for seeing strangers as gifts, in noticing that what comes from outside of itself may still be received. An enemy may yet speak a truth that I need to hear and consider. "[T]he adversary is part of my truth-finding process."[26] Even stronger, God may will that my life become bound up with my adversary such that my loving enemies is itself a crucial way of disclosing and revealing the truth about God and his world. God has provided the church in its sacramental life (though not only here) with the means to become well practiced in this skill.

Still, what are we to make of this "outside"? I mean simply outside the visible church, among those who do not claim to be Christians, in terms that are not always easily or self-evidently translatable into Christian language and symbols. In these remarks, I intend no diminishment of the ways that Christian language and symbols (and stories and rites) function in making possible the Christian life for those who endeavor to live it and even for those who do not, but nevertheless find themselves touched by it in one way or another. We learn how to give without expecting anything in return by "offering" our gifts (and our very selves) to God only to be met with the different and offset counter-gift of the feast of the Lamb. It goes without saying that it requires great faith to continue to pray and hope for things when it seems that God is not listening.

Even so, part of our learning—if we are in fact learning what we ought to—will be the dispositions and virtues necessary to handle the counter-gift's unpredictability. We will consign neither the gift nor the counter-gift to the strict logic of transaction. Nor will we guard the entire giving enterprise in the name of security (think of the ways that mortgage

---

26. Yoder, *Body Politics*, 69. Yoder is characterizing and agreeing with what Gandhi means by "experimenting with truth."

companies do this with borrowers—the opposite of gift and counter-gift).[27] We will set giving free from being rule governed in the interest of protection. In the interim between gift and counter-gift, we will instead display the waiting appropriate to a people who have learned to trust in promises that do not deliver on cue or ahead of (or on) schedule. Jesus, as God's gift and presence to his creation, does not act out the solution to a problem that humanity created in its sinful refusal in Adam. Jesus is not God's "reaction" to human sinfulness, a goodness in exact inverse to evil. But as unexpected counter-gift, he is God's excess that overflows the boundaries that humanity "creates" precisely because anything we create (even by our sinning) mysteriously finds itself *within* God's original gift and goodness. Jesus, in other words, is yet more of that goodness.[28] Therefore included in the very ways that these words and symbols function to create Christian worship, for example, is already the introduction of an expectation that does not spoil the surprise for which Christians are asked to wait. Consider the biblical example of the unlikely prophet Jonah.

Fleeing from God's presence and call, Jonah stirred the anger of the others on the boat who panicked at the storm. They cried, "What do you mean, you sleeper? Arise, call upon your god! Perhaps the god will give a thought to us, that we do not perish" (1:6). But later, Jonah is wide awake, watching for Nineveh's destruction and God's judgment on the city (4:5). In the first case, he may sleep because he misunderstands how God might judge a prophet whose effrontery attempts to escape the burden of his call. In the second case, he stays awake to witness something he was certain would occur, having himself declared it. But in both cases the prophet's relationship with the prophet's truth is misconstrued. Waking or sleeping, the true prophet is burdened with a message that he wishes would pass to someone else. He continually attempts to release it and often only bears it out of reluctance, despairing for having been chosen but nevertheless committed to the office.

It is quite the opposite for Jonah, whose evasion of the call is not just (or even primarily) seen when he boards a Tarshish-bound boat. His

27. The language of "economic security" comes to mind for how it elides questions of a household's or community's well-being in favor of warmed-over questions of violence disguised as the goods of national security.

28. This way of putting it is meant to confuse, appropriately, God's creating with God's giving of himself in Christ. It is *not* intended to imply that Christ is part of creation, but only to emphasize that both Christ and creation are gifts of abundance; both are acts of God.

actual pronouncement of God's judgment shows nothing of the appropriate prophetic reluctance.[29] He self-consciously grasps at the truth that he proclaims and is himself invested with the truth of words rather than the truth of the God whose prophet he is.

Jonah's determination to witness the destruction of Nineveh is therefore a microcosm of his entire unfaithfulness. His problem was not that God acted and he missed it because he was asleep. Instead, his wakefulness was suited to something he had decided ahead of time. His failure to wait for God to act was accomplished by waiting, though for the wrong thing. He waited for God to act *in this precise way*.[30] His watching was out of character to the God of Israel, who will show mercy to whom he will show mercy (Exod 33:19), and was instead more nearly suited to a god who could be known with greater precision than one who is living. Jonah's god, in other words, had become an idol. And one who waits wide awake for a dead god who acts on cue only waits for oneself dressed up as another. When his preaching goes unfulfilled, he despairs, not that it implies his service to a false god, but that he is himself full of contradictions, disconnected predictions and outcomes. Jonah wants to die (4:8) for exactly this reason. He fears being wrong more than he fears making an idol out of God.

What is the lesson of Jonah for wide-awake Christians? It illustrates something learned from Anselm (see chapter 4 below): knowing God's truth is bound up with knowing God as always present to his promises to knowers. God remains free. The truth about God is neither separate nor separable from God, and it cannot become so without becoming false. Jonah's prophesies turned out to be false—as he had feared—though not for the reasons he thought. He feared a God of contradiction, who does not follow through on threats, who evades the gravity of his own words. But God does not threaten destruction on the same logic as God's promises to save. Prophetic speech, if it is to be true, must always be spoken as God's saving words, *especially* when it looks as though they are obviously words

---

29. In fact, most of the prophets complain that nobody listens to them. In Jonah we see the confusion that sets in when they actually gain a hearing (cf. Jer 27:9).

30. An anecdote can remind us of the many ways that people use the Bible in order to make it relevant to contemporary situations. R. S. Sugirtharajah relates a 2002 letter to the editor of *The Guardian* that invokes the example of Jonah's already made-up mind in order to rebuke President Bush and Prime Minister Blair when both appeared eager to invade Iraq regardless of the outcome of UN weapons inspections. See Sugirtharajah, *Postcolonial Reconfigurations*, 77.

of judgment and condemnation. The one who is awake to God, therefore, is not one who is alert to the possibility that God may change his mind, but one who hopes for the day when words of judgment become words of good news and mercy. The prophet, in other words, gives up control over words out of expectation that they are in fact God's living diction of active, saving promise.

It is also important that Nineveh was "outside" to Jonah. (We might say that it was Israel's outside, her clear enemy, as evidenced by Nahum's prophecy.) This is surely the reason that Jonah had difficulty seeing the city's repentance as part of God's work. Not only had God become, for him, an idol in the sense of being imagined as operating according to pre-scripted formulae and therefore an inactive agent (a dead agent). But also, Jonah's God was smaller than the Lord of the Nations. He was, instead, lord of one nation, one that dispensed judgments disguised as calls to repent while the welcome was disingenuous. God would no more extend grace to Israel's enemies than he would make a covenant with them. Christianity (like Judaism, though differently at points) makes the astounding claim that "our God" is also God of the whole world, including of those who do not know him. This conviction underlies Paul's speech to the Athenians about their "unknown god" (Acts 17). Reading the story of Jonah thus prefigures the Christian inclusion of the Gentiles, that is, the gospel being news for all nations of the world. By definition, the Gentiles are "outside" to Israel. But the gospel's "innovation" (something that was not nearly as new as it may have seemed) was to narrate the fulfillment of God's promise to Abraham through Israel to every other nation. The gospel knows no "outside" since even the stranger has become a friend; the rigid boundaries that separated one people from another have been brought down. In Christ, the far-off have been brought near; aliens and strangers to God who have lived without hope have been brought within (Eph 2:14).

The Christian ability to see God outside the church is not a way of losing faith in the church—that is, in God's presence to and in the church as the body of Christ. It is precisely a confidence that the God who is present to the church has not left it to cope with empty promises and discouragement, nor with a charge and mission that it will not be able to accomplish. It is fundamentally a confession that God can be known as one whose love extends not only to the church but to the whole world.

chapter three

Surprise Made Flesh

God has touched the world during the world. The divine life intersects the life of creation in creation's time and, through its existence there, extends and grants it duration. This touch is most definitive in the incarnation. One way to think about the significance of the incarnation is to consider the difference between *giving* and *solidarity*. When you give, you make available to someone else something that you have that now is for them. God gave to Israel the Law and then sent his prophets to correct the sons and daughters of Israel when they became disobedient. Solidarity surpasses this. Solidarity is not giving what you have but giving *what you are*. In Christ, Christians believe, God gives himself to creatures in order to be with us, to suffer with us in our vulnerability to the crucifying world we have made for ourselves out of rebellion to the things and ways of God.

The incarnation of the Son of God is a surprise. Nothing in the whole of human history could have prepared us for it since even on this side of it, we are almost completely at a loss for how to talk about it. If the counterpoint to surprise is not ignorance but rather merely the lack of human foreknowledge, then there is no sufficient knowledge that precedes the coming of Jesus Christ. Yet this does not mean that there is no knowledge *at all* that precedes Jesus. There is, after all, a kind of preparation for Jesus' coming. The future coming of the Messiah was the topic of many of the messages Israel's prophets proclaimed. Isaiah told of a Servant of God who, despite his meekness and gentleness, would not be received and yet also would not tire of his mission until justice and righteousness are brought to the nations (Isaiah 42). Crucially, however, the knowledge that prophecy imparts is not yet itself an encounter with the content of prophecy. If prophetic knowledge were *sufficient* in this sense, then it would do in and for the present what can only be future.

In our own time, modern ways of knowing notoriously sought precisely this kind of collapse of the prophetic present into the future event when it attempted to circumscribe what could be known in advance of knowing it. This move reduces all knowledge to quantities that can be known ahead of their "discovery," a reduction that yielded some benefit for the modern mind. In particular, knowledges receive an implicit ordering and valuing such that general knowledge (at the "meta" level) ranks higher than specific knowledge. Categories become more important than those things that fill them. One reason it was so difficult for Jesus' contemporaries to recognize him as the promised Messiah is that "Messiah" functioned for them as a known quantity, a savior-king who would resemble David (and Moses and Joshua) and serve to bring prosperity and liberation to Israel, to restore glory to her worship, to reinvigorate the nation with piety and true religion, and to stamp out the Roman occupiers. These marks of the future hope must have seemed far-fetched, but we suspect that they surely would have been recognized if present. Trusting Israel's prophets when they spoke of the coming Messiah, then, required a great deal of hope. Yet it did not seem to require a great deal of knowledge since the ability to recognize the Messiah seemed to depend on categories and experiences that were already with the people to whom the Messiah was to come. And the past only requires *remembrance* for it to become present knowledge.

John the Baptist preached a message of repentance that would make ready the path for Jesus' arrival (Mark 1:2–8). It is anticipation and hope but not without preparation. John did not dispense a knowledge about who was coming, but only the challenge to prepare in order to be able to recognize him when he comes. He offered the mode of perception itself. We might say that John did not educate those who would hear concerning a "Christology"; rather, his message of repentance was a call to reorient one's vision so that the Messiah could be seen simply and plainly for who he is when he comes. John, in other words, did not spoil the surprise that the Messiah's coming always ultimately would be. He instead set about preparing Israel, as all of the prophets had done, to apprehend the work of God *as still* a surprise, something that will only be distinguished from the

Surprise Made Flesh

normal course of things (political troublemaker, good teacher) by those whose expectations are set beyond them.

How ought we to think about being trained for right seeing? What may we point to that forms people into those who will recognize the Son of God for who he is when he comes? How might they be prepared in advance to be those who exclaim without hesitation, "Behold the Lamb of God!"? It seems to me that there are at least three ways of seeing something, which I shall label the reporter, the voyeur, and the witness.

To a *reporter*—who acts much like a modern scientist, if you like—only the specific facts are in question. She may not herself be dispassionate about them, but she will generally strive for a certain degree of objectivity lest her work come to be labeled commentary and opinion. The reporter goes out to see what is there. The *voyeur*, on the other hand, knows what he goes out to see, wants to see it, and does. He is not disinterested but instead anticipates his seeing by *foreseeing*, even impatiently waiting on the arrival of what is already known and will only be added on to it as "experience." Like the reporter, finally, the *witness* is not quite sure what to expect but trusts that he will know it when it appears. Yet it is not a trust shared by the reporter. For the witness is caught in the difficult situation of waiting to see something that cannot be known except by seeing it.

Witness is tied to truth, whereas voyeurism is tied to satisfaction and gratification. This is because there is no discernible good that derives from the witnessed event that may be consumed, and this is further tied to the event's uniqueness since the truth is always unique. Someone may be pleased by the truth or horrified by it. And while it is true that horror may drive some to believe fantasies instead, fantasies cannot ever be said to yield witness (because a belief in fantasies always comes more readily than the moral determination of the witness to believe the truth). If the truth brings satisfaction to the witness, it is because the witness's love of truth is more basic than his love of pleasure.

Nietzsche parsed things differently, keenly aware of the human propensity to believe lies for the sake of the comfort they bring. We might say that he suspected all witness of voyeurism. Indeed, this has become a chief suspicion of our age, a great insight that acknowledges that the knower and the thing known are impossible to separate. The seer and the thing seen now mimic each other and throw light around each other, confusing and problematizing the ways that former philosophies managed to carry on assured of their own objectivity. In Nietzsche's words, "facts are precisely what there is not, only interpretations."[1] Our being in the world already includes ourselves in the things we see, which means that we cannot help imposing ourselves on them, especially when we *want* to see them, desiring to see particular things and not others. To Nietzsche, this reveals that our will is always more basic than our knowledge. "It is our needs that interpret the world; our drives and their For and Against. Every drive is a kind of lust to rule; each one has its perspective that it would like to compel all the other drives to accept as a norm."[2]

Yet the voyeur is also partly subject to this critique because the voyeur acts to insert distance between himself and the object of his vision: he is very often nothing but a Peeping Tom, leering from afar in the hopes of catching a glimpse of a misdeed or private moment meant for someone else. Such lookers take what does not belong to them in what Thomas Nagel describes as an "incomplete relation," its acting according to the spirit of consumption where the availability of anything presents itself for being devoured by mere vision. It is precisely the consumability of the thing seen that tells us that it stands alienated, preyed upon by a ravenous indifference. "A voyeur," writes Nagel, "need not require any recognition by his object at all."[3] The voyeur sees what does not welcome it; he is not only not invited, but indeed even requires the very privacy he violates. It is not possible to steal and to gain possession of something that is already available and at hand. Remoteness, we might say, is the very condition for this kind of seeing. Noninvolvement is simply preserved by the covert voyeur's ways; anonymity and a silent self maintain the security and sanctity of a knowledge attained with uttermost cleanliness. It is like those time travelers who journey to the past and observe themselves, taking great care not to intervene out of fear of altering the future.[4] However,

---

1. Nietzsche, *Will to Power*, sec. 481.
2. Ibid.
3. Nagel, "Sexual Perversion," 134.
4. Jean-Paul Sartre reflects on a situation in which a voyeur is discovered, thus forcing the voyeur now to recognize himself as a being given the recognition by the Other. This exposes the voyeur's putative freedom from the demands placed by a vision that sees without being seen. "Strictly speaking, it is not that I perceive myself losing my freedom

for the voyeur, *every* possible future demands such care. Knowledge cannot be touched without implicating the toucher in the future of the thing touched. The voyeur "has" his object to the same degree that it remains just beyond his grasp.

> The theologian cannot be a passive voyeur, a casual tourist surveying the landscape of tradition. The philosopher or the historian of religion can stand outside the arena of his or her inquiry as a disinterested observer. For the theologian, however, commitment precedes inquiry. Experience of the life of faith and participation in a faith community anticipates theological investigation.[5]

Yet if we are honest, we know this is not always the Christian reality. Consider the *Christian voyeur*—one who refuses all participation, one who wants belief without being discovered, as it were. It is one who wants to know without being known.[6] If there is such a thing, the Christian voyeur likely lives an un-liturgical Christian existence, as Catherine Pickstock argued in her essay "Liturgy and Modernity."[7] Such a Christian is thoroughly modern, wanting to see without the work of actual engagement. Life is characterized by *disconnection*—life from work, work from faith, public from private. Against this, the structure of liturgy enacts a cadence for all living (as opposed to watching). It patterns life for the Christian believer and Christian community with appropriate temporal beats of memory and anticipation. The future never becomes for us a knowledge that is able to be sundered from the hope required to continue to believe the promises according to which we find the strength to wait for it. The "it" that the future is can never be more sure than the promise that delivers it, otherwise the future would already in a sense be entirely available to us. Likewise, the past is kept alive through memory, prevented from turning into the cold, dead stuff of an orphaned history, stories that continue to be told by people who tell them as somebody else's, but without a real stake in telling them truthfully. This is the reason

---

in order to become a *thing*, but my nature is—over there, outside my lived freedom—as a given attribute of this being which I am for the Other" (*Being and Nothingness*, 263).

5. Sherwin, *Faith Finding Meaning*, 51–52.

6. In her exposition of theological themes in Milton, Regina M. Schwartz notes that scopophilia (voyeurism) generates and depends on a form of knowledge that is characteristic of Satan: stolen rather than given, aggressive, and seeking to master as one surveys prey (*Remembering and Repeating*, 53–59).

7. Pickstock, "Liturgy and Modernity," esp. 23–24.

that liturgy must be practiced, just as it also matters who practices it. Liturgy functions to unite the church with Christ, bringing together, for example, the Christ of the post-resurrection accounts with Christ who is risen and present to the world, to and as the church eucharistically. (I treat in chapter 7 the manner of Christ's eucharistic presence to the church.) When Christians remember the death of Jesus through their liturgical actions, these actions become present Christian living that not only guide the church in discerning the good and looking for the work of God's kingdom outside the church; astonishingly they are actually themselves already these very things.

These are claims that call out for expansion and elaboration. At the least, I am convinced that they suggest a radical and irreducible *provisionality* to the work of Christians when they take part in liturgical acts. This may be refracted in at least two senses. First, liturgy is not preparation for something that comes later. It is neither a summary nor a survey. It does not enumerate the most salient points of the plot apart from the contours of the plotlines themselves, nor does it sift away the chaff of real history in order to be left with the wheat of the most earnest and essential principles. This is why the Christian creeds must ultimately be prayed in order to be true. As prayers, they plead for God to provide the faith to believe *in* rather than simply believe *that*.[8] These should not be thought mutually exclusive since, in specifying the identity of the God in whom Christians ask for the faith to believe, they are also asking for the faith to believe that these things truly identify this God.

Creeds are not meant to be summaries of the Christian message or substitutes for the narrative history to which that message is inextricably joined. We may therefore be fairly relaxed about the fact that most of the creeds we have do not deal with Jesus' life, but skip directly from the virgin birth to his passion. Clearly the life of Jesus is important, but creeds were never meant to give us a summary of every serious Christian theme or part of the narrative.[9] Christians believe in the incarnation of

---

8. Adams, "Reasoning in Tradition," 209–22.

9. Noting also the absence of reference to the Old Testament narrative, Jenson suggests an additional phrase: "The time of creed making is in most churches' and theologians' judgment finished, but as a hypothesis contrary to fact, one can think of a creed whose second article would have begun, 'and in Jesus Christ, his only Son, our Lord, who as the Word given to Moses led Israel out of Egypt...'" (*Canon and Creed*, 30–31). I recall a Mennonite theologian at a conference suggesting the addition of something like "he preached peace and justice." Even if it is an omission, one way to respond to it is simply

Surprise Made Flesh

Christ, for example, as following a narrative course of events in real history, though it is not only a history as it has been produced by a series of antecedent causes or even one simply yielding a main event that has received its proper and lengthy introduction. Instead, confessing the creeds exercises the first and decisive step in the Christian will to embody truths that are also mysteries, and as such will not bear being rendered a knowledge other than the kind that is only had by catching up the confessor in the life of its truth.[10]

This leads to the second accent of provisionality: it is obvious but also crucial that all of these things take time to do. They are thus provisional in the sense of awaiting and striving for a completion that can come in no other way than through taking the time required to enact the work of the church's liturgy. They are not "given" in a completed transaction, nor do they court a panoply of options through which the same "effects" may be gained by other multiple means, means that may take less time or no time at all. In fact, the time liturgy takes is irreducible—it cannot be speeded up or lost without undoing itself. Its pace also paces our lives. What liturgy "does" can only be accomplished in its performance and is not an intrinsic element of, say, the liturgical *texts*.[11] Texts will be "used," but their use will connote how they are being *performed* rather than *consumed*. The texts only have their full meaning when tied to the experiences they enable. So the history to which the Christian confession of the incarnation refers is not permitted to be a history other than the one that includes the time that it takes to make the very confession. When Christians confess that God became a man, in other words, the fact that confessing it beats along in a liturgical rhythm unites the Christian to God's incarnating action in time and, just so, it is prayer.[12] As prayer, it is more hope than

---

to observe the difficulty in boiling down the life of Jesus to a single phrase. This is not unique to Jesus, but to every human life.

10. I do not mean to imply an absurdity such as that our believing it makes it true, or even that our wills are conditions of its truth. The will to believe the truth is, in an obviously existential sense, more fundamental than truth. But more to the point here is simply that the truth that is God in Christ generates a life, and it is just so a life that we inhabit through that kind of belief, hope, trust, and so on that prayer uniquely is.

11. It is good to remember that the psalms, and indeed all of Scripture, are liturgical texts and so in this precise way also resist reduction to ahistorical forces. Movements within Christian thought that objectify the Bible are generally attempts to render the church redundant.

12. We might therefore rightly conceive of prayer as the human action that forms the

knowledge, more an act of dependence on the content of the confession and its specific truth than an assertion of theological theorems. Here we may identify the precise pathology of the voyeur as consumption without change, use without alteration. The voyeur opens everything except himself. Even his "seeing" is nonsensual. It is disembodied since ultimately nothing passes beyond the eyes. It is a "mere appearance" that coolly apprehends and assesses even while the voyeur cannot, in the end, actually see beauty since the voyeur cannot love. Objects parade before a passive gaze but are not drawn toward the lookers.

Against this, the time that liturgy requires therefore reflects the *historic* nature of Christianity. It keeps Christians who participate in it from supposing that the gospel is a set of facts about God or enlightened information that must be consumed. Instead, the gospel must be *received*.[13] Its reception is temporally extended; when it comes, it comes in time. It is neither a philosophy nor a code of living. It is rather the report of contingent, historical occurrences. There is little use, for example, in speculating about how the gospel would be different if it had been centered in another culture at another time, whether its main currents had gone to the east and south rather than primarily west and north, whether God had chosen to create a people other than Israel or no people at all, whether he had decided not to speak through prophets but instead somehow to speak unmediated to the populations of earth all at once.

These are all unanswerable questions because, whatever else it happens to be, Christianity always carries its history. Perhaps most fundamentally it speaks of God's history with humanity, and like it or not, this history really is one way rather than another in the same way that it continues to be written in some ways and not others. This highlights the way that the gospel is therefore not something that can be deduced from more basic principles and theorems just as its proper transmission and enactment resists its being reduced to these things. When Christian apologists have felt anxiety or embarrassment over the particularity of the story the gospel tells and is, this has been because they have really preferred a timeless Jesus, one who is no more tied to Palestine in the first century than to any other place and any other time. They supposed that

---

inverse of God's kenosis, though only an "inverse" that depends on God being in Christ and in time *first* and as the fullness of prayer's possibility.

13. Jenson, *Systematic Theology*, 1:168: "[T]he proclamation is itself contingent; as news, it cannot be deduced or summoned but only received when and if it comes."

what makes the gospel "for us" is its ability to shed its particular content, to be universal in this sense. They sought a status of "for everyone at all times" for the gospel—not as a genuine refusal to think of the Lord as a tribal deity, but as a refusal to consider the particularities of Jesus' history to be decisive.[14] Yet this is merely a longing for a disembodied gospel and a Christ without incarnation.

Moreover, it is a longing for a church without witness. The activity of witness is a historic one that depends on continuity with the past. Those who have not themselves seen what the eyewitnesses saw nevertheless believe them. Their faith in the gospel's truth is thus partly a faith in the church in its earlier generations, a trust in those who carried that testimony into the future. This is not to say that there are two acts of faith—one in God's gospel and one in the truthfulness of the church's message throughout time. These two things are really one thing, two aspects of it: the truth of the gospel that today's Christians believe includes the true witness of the church. This is the reason that the tradition's dogmas persist throughout the history of the church. When councils settled questions about Christology and the Trinity, they intended for their decisions to be irreversible. Jenson distinguishes doctrine from dogma in this respect: "A dogmatic choice is one by which the church so decisively determines her own future that if the choice is wrongly made, the community determined by that choice is no longer in fact the community of the gospel; thus no church thereafter exists to reverse the decision."[15]

As a consequence, argues Jenson, *that* a church continues to exist, embodying and sustaining the dogma produced by previous generations, attests to the adequacy of those dogmatic choices inasmuch as what was at stake in the formulation of dogma is in fact the church's continued existence. Even so, to affirm this is not to retreat into the safety of a timeless existence. It is not even to vindicate the decisions of our forebears in the faith on the basis of the church's empirical existence, since what we call church may really turn out to be a false community and a self-deluded parody of the true gospel. The point is that earlier dogmatic decisions were so determinative of the church's existence that a false church became the only other possibility. "Therefore, to believe that the entity which now calls

---

14. This modern strategy was followed in many forms. Immanuel Kant followed it in ethics and theologians followed it in various versions up through and beyond Rudolf Bultmann.

15. Jenson, *Systematic Theology*, 1:17.

itself the Christian church is the church of the apostles and to believe that the church's past dogmatic decisions were adequate to their purposes—not necessarily in every way appropriate to them—comes to the same thing." For example, Jenson suggests that if Nicea's formulation of Christ as "of one being with the Father" was not actually true to the gospel, then the council was so committing itself in its decision to use that formulation that those who followed them in confessing it do not simply place themselves outside the church in doing so, but their confession marks the nonexistence of any church. In Jenson's words, if it was a formulation false to the gospel, "the gospel was thereby so perverted that there has since been no church extant to undo the error."[16]

This is one way to affirm that the timefulness of the gospel—the way that God meets the world in Christ—is not limited to the time of Jesus in his first-century Palestinian ministry and passion in Jerusalem. The gospel in time also includes the church's own real history. If dogma is "timeless" in the sense that Jenson describes as definitional, it is only able to be so because it is so clearly the result of the church's own work to resolve theological dilemmas and questions *in time*. As it is, those who abjure the church's tradition in favor of its present existence deny the gospel's embodiment. We might say that a disembodied "gospel" longs for no church, each generation wanting to secure its belief through its own experience, appealing to its direct encounter with God apart from a church that persists through historic continuity. But this distorts the kind of "experience" the gospel promises as part of its authentic reception in time, which I described above as its liturgical participation. Indeed, a high regard for the temporal is partly what unites liturgy with regard for the church's tradition, a point that is evidenced by the fact that they tend to be either both present or both absent, depending on the ecclesial tradition.

Crucial to an adequate account of the incarnation, then, are not only christological questions, but corresponding ecclesiological ones. The theological skill and sensibility required for narrating Christ in the world as the very work of God is subtle and neither easily nor quickly achieved. When Christians take seriously their role as witnesses rather

---

16. Ibid. An objection that appears obvious is to point to the existence of churches that do not abide by decisions made at Nicea. If errors were made, might these churches undo them? But Jenson's point is that Nicea's decisiveness made no allowance for this and that the fact that they did not reveals a lot about how the church was understood to be embodied historically.

Surprise Made Flesh

than voyeurs, they submit themselves to the discipline necessary to this theological skill and sensibility. Indeed, such submission is already an act of training to the extent that the vision of the witness must partly be shaped by the attestations of those whose seeing preceded ours.

The Christian attempt to avoid the work of witness is too easily satisfied with knowing rather than participating. What is "known" does not finally affect the body since its rough corners have already been knocked off. Such things can *only* be known this way—simplified, rarefied, purified. There is little room for surprise, only an exact correspondence between what one sets out to see and what one ends up seeing. Nothing new intrudes on the voyeur's vision; there are only replays of anticipated images. The gospel may be *understood*, then, but not *received*. But this is surely a hopeless gospel since so long as the gospel is *simply* understood, it is not in fact understood at all since the gospel is crucially a *life* (John 10:10). Life can only be received and it will only be experienced in time and over time. Jesus, then, whose very incarnation is a life with our own, must likewise be received, not simply believed or understood (John 1:11).

It is worth considering how the traditional way Christians refer to "receiving" the Eucharist preserves this insight. Perhaps the Eucharist is more obviously *bodily* than *temporal*. Its characteristic *sensuality* communicates the body that it is to and for the body that it creates in its celebration—the ecclesial body that displays and enacts its utter dependence on the body of Christ given and received. But already, then, this bodily communication denotes distinct beats that are separated in times, the separation between the giving and the receiving, the promising and the fulfilling, the speaking and the creating. Its temporality is central to its reception since anything received must first be given and it goes without saying that all giving takes place in time.[17] When the priest gives the Eucharist, the Eucharist sacramentally reenacts God's giving of Christ to the world which "received him not" (John 1:11) and as such re-invites the world to the feast that all of humanity has already, in fact, refused to attend. God refuses our refusal in Christ with a re-giving that rebuffs death's finality with resurrection's re-gift. The invitation is thus reissued.

---

17. In theology, recent reflections on the anthropology of "the gift"—drawing on the work of anthropologist Marcel Mauss—have observed this, particularly in the need for some time to elapse between gift and counter-gift lest the counter-gift be perceived to be a refusal, an immediate giving back. On this topic, see, in particular, Milbank, "Can a Gift be Given?"

Anticipating chapter 5, we may therefore say that, because of this, the resurrection is God's final act with creation since it is not controlled by death, creation's other end. It is not, that is to say, purposed *within* creation but is the end to creation that God adds through the person and work of Christ.

Many have misunderstood the Eucharist's temporality, especially in how it recapitulates Christ's sacrifice.[18] The Reformation preference for the language of "table" over "altar" intends to avoid a Eucharist that *repeats* Christ's sacrifice. In an extreme version, this avoidance completely denies any connection with that one-time sacrifice except through the act of remembrance. But catholic thought can affirm the reenactment of Christ's sacrifice without its repetition by a sacramental union of the passion of Christ with the church's existence as Christ's present body within the world.[19] The church may reenact the sacrifice of Christ since its involvement in its ritual performance itself *constitutes* and builds up the church as the body of Christ. Put differently and from the opposite side of the logic, perhaps only to the extent that the church fails to see that it is eucharistically made will it feel the need to take drastic measures to ensure that the ritual does nothing at all.[20] As I argued in the preceding chapter, this is an anxiety of overidentifying Christ with the church, something a more adequate understanding of the sacraments—one that insists on their mysteriousness—in fact avoids.

We may at least suspect that the temporal extension of sacramental enactment introduces the church to (and prepares the church for) a life of waiting that nevertheless is not paralyzed through inactivity. The Christian life is probably best understood as one of waiting, receiving, giving thanks, and hoping even while it is also just as often one of waiting and hoping without receiving or knowing exactly how to give thanks for those things hoped for. The time that hoping and waiting take, we might say, themselves have a ritual shape or cadence since the ritual actions are

---

18. Cf. Calvin, *Institutes of the Christian Religion*, IV.18.

19. This view was affirmed by the Council of Trent (1545–1563).

20. Some will think that this way of putting the matter seems backward, but it is by no means clear to me which comes first: the denial of sacramentality of the ritual that leads to a view of the church that is ultimately alienated from the sacrament (such that, to be sure, the church loses all of its own sacramental character); or the church, in telling another story of its constitution and its being sustained, can no longer support a sacramental ritual that it would perhaps under other circumstances have wanted to maintain.

Surprise Made Flesh

likewise a determination to act in the face of God's promises rather than succumb to petrifying fear, which is loss of hope.

Having already addressed the liturgy and the manner in which its exercise crucially takes time, we can add a final aspect to it. The gospel's temporality—the fact, again, that it takes time—is, in some sense, nothing less than the gospel itself. Our refusal of God might have ended the time of God's giving of himself. If left to our own successes in rejecting God's act to be with us in Christ, the life of God would not be one that we could timefully live. Nevertheless, God has held time open and pushed back the end of all things. This is the preeminent work of the resurrection, since the way that the world "received him not" was not only displayed in the lack of welcome surrounding Jesus' birth in Bethlehem or in the fact that he was sometimes refused in Galilean towns where there was "nowhere to lay his head" (Luke 9:58). These only anticipated the world's ultimate failure to welcome him, which is to say its failure of *reception*—the cross. The resurrection re-gifts Christ to the world and so remakes history by the fact that this re-gifting takes time; the resurrection both creates the time for re-giving and is itself the repeated gift. It bears pointing out, then, that incarnation and resurrection not only share the status of gift but are in some sense the same gift, an identity that is only possible so long as the time that separates them is also given.

Up to this point, I have been focusing on how Jesus comes to our world and on the human ways of either avoiding or taming this surprising reality. Only witnesses can see Jesus as Lord. It is a confession that reduces Jesus neither to an object nor to an experience. I now want to consider a parallel to this by looking at another way that Jesus Christ is incarnate in the world. It is what I will call the extension of the incarnation as the church's proclamation.

The Prologue of John's Gospel audaciously re-narrates creation with the central character now made explicit. Jesus is the Word of God and is therefore something that God speaks. He is not reduced to the effects he produces, such as his words or his actions and miracles—these are not the Word that God speaks.[21] Rather God crucially speaks Jesus himself as

---

21. See Jenson, *Systematic Theology*, vol. 1, ch. 10.

the Son of God. God's speech to the world is his Son. The Son is thus, in a sense, God's diction and so, we might even say, *his liturgy* (or theurgy). If, as Nicene Christian thought maintains, the Trinity is God's supreme act of self-love and if creation is also an act of love (and does not arise from, say, need), then the love that creates is in fact the superabundance of this same divine self-love.

This means that creation is an intra-Trinitarian loving act. The love of the Father for the Son, as Augustine famously formulated (and the Catholic Church teaches), *is* the Holy Spirit, though we are justified in speaking of that love as itself a divine person due to its intensity and nature. The persons of the Trinity are what they are because their relations are, in a sense, more fundamental than their existence simply as such.[22] Yet now we can reverse this seeming separation between the work of God and the witness of Christ. If God's works, in a sense, proclaim themselves, then the work of witnesses is brought within God's own work. Might we even say that it is itself God's very work? If so, it will be so in a way that does not obviate human witness. God can and does witness to himself in the Word of the Son, and yet witness is also God's creative work within creation to join with the speech that the Son of God is as the divine Word.

Witness is given. But the phenomenon of witness is not simply to be identified with the resurrection. Rather the God who proclaims the Word to creation in the resurrected Christ (indeed *as* the resurrected Christ) gives that resurrection to witnesses as the only thing that makes possible the proclamation that witnesses will themselves speak. Likewise, we must not imagine that the words of worship, when human creatures utter them, are really (simply and straightforwardly) God's Word.[23] God's spoken word is not put in our mouths in this way as prophecy is, a message formed on human lips and yet with God's very authority. Something different occurs when the church, as Christ's very body, speaks about him. Worship is not prophecy, and prophets do not speak liturgies when they speak as prophets. In contrast, as the appropriate response of those parts of creation with speech to the speech that creates, liturgy returns speech to God, re-gifting the Logos. In worship, Christians therefore demonstrate their belief that a gift once given and refused nevertheless is still available for re-giving, which is another way of saying that, without resurrection,

---

22. See Augustine, *De Trinitate*, VII.1.2.

23. Though Barth rightly spoke of preaching as one of the three forms of the Word of God in *Church Dogmatics* I.1 and especially in I.2.

the words of liturgy not only can do no work but will literally have no words. Apart from God raising Jesus from the dead, there is no living word, and therefore nothing to speak, no gift to give back—the universe gone utterly mute and silent.

We should pause over what is potentially a theological problem here, particularly as orthodox Christianity has long refused to think of the Son as a part of creation. This was most notable in response to Arius. The Word that the Son is must therefore be thought as Word that "creates" a future in which the Son is determinative. But it must do so without making the Son a creature and thus a feature of the world. This can only happen so long as the future created by God's address in the Son *belongs* to the Son, which is to say it is the Son's future. Put differently, the Son does not inhabit the future of creation in the incarnation, entering the time of the world. But because the Son is in fact the agent and recipient of creation, then the future (as all time) is his. The so-called Cosmic Christ of Colossians comes to mind as an indication of how the New Testament itself appears to struggle with the relationship between Christ and creation:

> He is the image of the invisible God, the first-born of all creation; for in him all things were created, in heaven and on earth, visible and invisible, whether thrones or dominions or principalities or authorities—all things were created through him and for him. He is before all things, and in him all things hold together. (Col 1:15–17)

The more Christ is an indisputable agent of creation, the easier it is to fend off tendencies to speak of him as a creature. Yet the tendency persists because God's presence is so acutely *with, to,* and *among* creation in Christ. Just how so? What we call history is simply the time of his existence. Jesus Christ not only appears in the midst of human history; he literally makes such history possible by being to creation its own history. And since by the resurrection his life is still a going concern, the Son's future is not only the future of creation, but it is also God's own future. Christ is one with the world by being to it and in its midst an aspect of its unfinished character. Therefore, though it is common to insist that what makes God unique and therefore distinct from creatures is that his existence is, in fact, necessarily his essence rather than a property that creatures have, God's *actual* existence is bound up with Jesus and so also with creatures. Creation cannot, therefore, contemplate God as God without contemplating Jesus, God's being with us in time and "in" creation.

The Word of God does not simply describe something else, but (to borrow from analytic philosophy of language) it "performs" an action and constitutes an event. There is no prior and separate entity that exists to which the Word of God refers, nothing that can be known in this way without being spoken of and, even more significantly, being itself spoken. The Son is the Father's eternal utterance; there was never a time when God was without his Word. The "spoken of" quality of the Word is simply its being spoken by God. Here it is possible to see how the church's mission of proclamation is united with the spoken-ness of what it proclaims. When the church proclaims the gospel, in some way we must say that the Word of God is spoken, indeed is being re-spoken by the church to the world, even *into* the world. It is thus incarnated again and again, and its ability to be so is its original spoken-ness by God. The future created by God's speaking the Word is filled with speaking the Word.

The Word of God is event-making precisely in its opening up a future for both God and creation that is God's very self as Jesus. Christian faith in Jesus is then a faith that God's future will be gift exactly to the extent that Jesus too is gift. In giving Jesus, God gives creation its future. There is no "creation" without Jesus, and it is only idleness to ask what this would even mean since we cannot actually speak about eternity apart from history. This is not because history is a necessary part of God's being; Christian thought has always rejected the idea that creation (and so history) exists out of necessity—only God exists necessarily. Instead, the reason that eternity and history are properly spoken together is that God may only be identified by his presence in and to history. This is the case both with how creatures identify God (since for creatures God is never less than creator) and with how God identifies himself. This last point needs to be explained. In fact, it follows exactly from the fact that God is not only Trinity "with us" as if he may somehow be something other than Trinity "in himself." This is a disastrous separation that can only be sustained so long as God is continuously thought to be escaping from creation rather than the reverse, which is the gospel itself. Not only are we confronted in Christ with a God who is "with us" but crucially also with the creation now eschatologically taken "into God." What is eschatological about it is found in a decidedly *temporal* future, not a withdrawal into the inviolability of eternity. Everlasting life with God is a timeful, and so eminently human, way of living.

Surprise Made Flesh

I have been pursuing a train of thought that unites both the incarnation and the resurrection. A subsequent chapter will take up the question of what kind of gift the resurrection is, why it is a surprise, and how it continues to surprise even those who proclaim it. Here we can indicate that the future filled by the church's present speaking of the Word made possible by God's original speaking of the Word, the Son, points to the resurrection as a life that re-gifts the incarnation of Christ. Even more, the gifting of the Word is, in fact, the *speaking* of the Word, meaning that the incarnation and resurrection both "proclaim" Christ *themselves*, apart from the work that those who witness to them go on to do. Just as the rocks that would cry out in praise if the people were overwhelmed with reasons to be silent (Luke 19:40), all of creation is a work of God whose very existence proclaims God's greatness. Preeminently as Word, the works of God as speech in and as the Son are not only an "address" to the world, but are also themselves proclamations of the greatness of the works that they themselves are. Put simply, when Jesus declared that the kingdom of God is at hand (e.g., Mark 1:15), it was "at hand" by both pointing to Jesus himself among us and also, crucially, to Jesus as indeed himself the very declaration of the kingdom and so, as declaration, the reality of the kingdom.

This is one way to talk about how the kingdom of God is both already come and yet to come, just as this is the reality of Jesus himself who has come and yet will, as the Nicean creed affirms, "come again in glory to judge the living and the dead." The return of Christ brings the kingdom in its fullness by establishing God's rule over everything—and not just, as now, over those who hear his declaration of the kingdom. This is not to say that Jesus is not now Lord over all that is, but that God's address in Jesus is still a going concern, begun in Jesus' ministry around Galilee, entrusted to the church at Pentecost, and carried forth by its witnesses. Jesus is not only spoken *of*, but in a crucial sense, *is himself spoken* when witnesses speak. As Jesus' reign extends throughout the world through the work of witness, the incarnation comes more fully to instantiate the completeness of the kingdom that is first and only ever God's address to the world. Witnesses "incarnate" Jesus in their address to the world. This comes about not simply by preaching a message of repentance similar to the one Jesus himself preached, but by allowing their preaching to be God's continual proclamation.

God speaks in the speaking witness of the church just to the extent that the Son of God became human and, once more, to the same extent that the Spirit of God enables the church's speech. Consider the gift of tongues. The tongues are word, speech, and address. They must not only be *given* as the Father gives the Son (and so also the Father gives the Spirit), but they must also *be* the Spirit of Christ such that the Spirit does not give something other than himself. And exactly in giving himself he is giving Christ. The "reception" by the church is characterized by this same duality: the giving *of* the Spirit of Christ *by* the Spirit is not met by a body of people who receive anything external to themselves. Their receiving actually makes them a body in the spirit of Christ, which is to say, the church is *created* both by and as God's address. This is only a slightly different way of saying that the church is an extension of the incarnation.

chapter four

Free in Death

"What did we do when we unchained this earth from its sun?"[1]

Jesus did not want to die. In the garden of Gethsemane he prayed against a fate that was all but certain. In the course of this prayer, though, he committed himself to remaining faithful to the kind of living that would lead to his death. Nor did the Father want him to die. "Not my will but yours be done" (Luke 22:42, NRSV) should not be read as a disagreement or conflict of desires within the life of the Trinity. The historic debate about Christ's two wills in parallel to his two natures—human and divine—led some to propose the idea of monothelitism for fear that these wills might potentially conflict. When a seventh-century Council condemned the idea, it did so on grounds that there is no conflict. Christ's unity is preeminently shown in the fact that Christ's human will neither resists nor opposes the divine will. The Father and Son were in perfect agreement in not willing that the Son should undergo death at the hands of his enemies; the Son freely chose not to allow his own fear of death to overcome what was entailed in faithfully living to extremity.[2] On this, the Father and the Son were also in perfect agreement.

---

1. Nietzsche, *Gay Science*, sec. 125. Alasdair MacIntyre means something similar by what he calls an "epistemological crisis." See his "Epistemological Crises."

2. As N. T. Wright explains, "There have been many in the history of the world and the church who, not desiring to die for its own sake, have continued as a matter of integrity and vocation to follow the course on which they were set, knowing that this might, or

69

Yet how free was Jesus to do anything different? It is worth dwelling on the question of Christ's freedom, particularly at this pivotal moment in the gospel story, since too much Christian thinking has threatened to erase or subordinate it under the idea of *necessity*. There are good, biblical reasons that the idea that Jesus *had to die* is so common. The Gospels seem to show that this was Jesus' own understanding of the purpose for his life. For example, following Peter's confession that Jesus is the Messiah, Jesus tempers the mood by warning the disciples that "the Son of man must suffer many things, and be rejected by the elders and the chief priests and the scribes, and be killed, and after three days rise again" (Mark 8:31; cf. John 3:14). In the post-resurrection reality, two unnamed disciples on the Emmaus road tell Jesus, whom they do not recognize, how distraught they are that the one they had hoped would restore Israel had failed and, even worse, the grave did not contain the body. Jesus replies, "Was it not *necessary* that the Christ should suffer these things and enter into his glory?" (Luke 24:26, emphasis added). Likewise, the idea appears in Peter's Pentecost sermon: "this Jesus, delivered up according to the definite plan and foreknowledge of God, you crucified and killed by the hands of lawless men" (Acts 2:23).

How should we understand this necessity and this concept of God's definite plan? Is it at odds with Jesus' freedom to act and even to surprise? In the case of the Emmaus disciples, we get the sense that they should have known better, that they should have recognized Jesus, if they had understood better the way that Jesus fulfilled the Scriptures about Israel's hope for the Messiah. It is true that they *did* have expectations for the Messiah, for the way that he would deliver Israel. Their problem was not a failure of expectation, but of interpretation (v. 27). They interpreted the death of Jesus as the collapse of their hopes. Was this how they failed to recognize Jesus as the Messiah? Should they instead have seen his death as the act by which God was restoring Israel? Or ought their expectation simply to have outlived the crucifixion? If Jesus were really the Messiah of God, should the disciples have clung to this conviction *despite his death*, continuing to believe that God was in fact still going to deliver Israel *through him*? I think the latter is most likely. But then is this way of speaking of *necessity* too idiosyncratic and forced? Again, the larger question

---

even would inevitably, result in their deaths, and being ready to interpret that, too, as part of the same integrity and vocation" (Borg and Wright, *Meaning of Jesus*, 99).

Free in Death

has to do with the freedom of Jesus in his death: could he still be free if everything that transpired was the unfolding of God's plan?

There is at least a problem here if it is also the case that Christ "became obedient unto death" (Phil 2:9). We may not think much of an action one undergoes if one does it just because one has to, and we will not typically call it *obedience*—perhaps simply *acquiescence* to another. We generally assume freedom is required in order for that person to be praised for being obedient. Yet Paul is here invoking Jesus' obedience and humility as a model for how Christians ought to live, something that only works if Jesus was free from necessity. It is crucial that Jesus went to his death voluntarily and that God in Christ was acting freely and not from any compulsion in undergoing the suffering for which Christianity has learned to speak with gratitude. Thomas Aquinas clarifies this by appealing to several different ways that Aristotle teaches it is possible to speak of the meaning of necessity. One that he rules out completely is what he calls the necessity of compulsion:

> a thing may be necessary from some cause quite apart from itself; and should this be either an efficient or a moving cause then it brings about the necessity of compulsion; as, for instance, when a man cannot get away owing to the violence of someone else holding him. . . . It was not necessary, then, for Christ to suffer from necessity of compulsion, either on God's part, who ruled that Christ should suffer, or on Christ's own part, who suffered voluntarily.[3]

What then is a better way to think about this necessity? Thomas speaks of the suffering of Christ in the same terms that he speaks of the incarnation and the resurrection: in terms of its fittingness or *convenientia*.[4] Hebrews 2:10 uses this language: "For it was *fitting* that he, for whom and by whom all things exist, in bringing many sons to glory, should make the pioneer of their salvation perfect through suffering" (emphasis added). As I will discuss in chapter 5, Thomas makes use of this concept in order to talk, after the fact, about how something gathers together a number of diverse elements (*convenientia* literally means to come together). They do not make sense on their own, but only collectively and after the fact can it be seen that their unity is somehow appropriate, even aesthetically pleasing. So Christ's suffering "was necessary from necessity of the end

---

3. Aquinas, *Summa Theologica*, III.46.1 (this notation refers to the third part, question 46, article 1).

4. Ibid., III.46.1–3.

proposed."⁵ And if there are multiple ends, then it is "convenient" (a form of necessity) that he suffered if his suffering gathers the ends together in the best way.⁶ For example, John 3:14 teaches that "as Moses lifted up the serpent in the wilderness, so must the Son of man be lifted up." Following Thomas's distinction, the sense here of "must" is supplied by end-necessity rather than compulsion-necessity. This in fact seems clear from the next clause: "that whoever believes in him may have eternal life" (v. 15). What is necessary or must happen is not an external limitation on God's freedom nor compulsion against it, but a free choice to seek the end of eternal life of human creatures.⁷

Does this help? I think that it does since it at least keeps us focused on the *goals* of Jesus' actions rather than seeing his actions as the goals themselves. Put differently, Jesus endures the cross for purposes other than simply dying. We may genuinely speak about Jesus' actions in going to the cross as obedience, compelled by an end that faithfulness required in order to get there.

The cross is appropriately spoken of as a great Christian mystery that, for many, accurately confesses our confusion when confronted with the question about how it *works*. Christianity has long confessed that the cross has something intrinsically to do with the reconciliation between God and sinners. Yet there is a significant sense in which it is not mysterious at all. It is the most natural thing you would expect for one who insists on living a fully human life in front of a world that thrives on and rewards inhumanity. Reflecting on the panoply of questions surrounding the cross, Dominican theologian Herbert McCabe considers those who ask, "Why did Jesus decide to be crucified? What was the reason for the cross? Why something so strange as the crucifixion for the Son of God?" In response, McCabe teaches:

> Now my belief is that the ordinary Christians who have kept the crucifix or the sign of the cross as their creed . . . never had this problem at all. The ordinary people, deep down in their understanding have never had the slightest puzzle about the cross. They have taken it for granted. Why naturally the man was crucified.

---

5. Ibid., III.46.1.

6. It is odd to speak about *any* suffering as convenient, but this is a case where Latin connotes differently from English.

7. In highlighting this distinction, Thomas follows Aristotle's well-known distinction between an efficient cause (here, *compulsion*) and a final cause (here, *end*).

Free in Death

Aren't we all? Whether they would put it into words or not, they felt deep down that crucifixion really does express what life is about. It is not a thing that is easily acknowledged; for one thing it is something we are afraid to face—that the deep things in life are suffering and death.[8]

Yet pronouncing the cross as in any way a sanguine memory is something that Christianity is enabled and ennobled to confess only after the Father pronounces judgment on the cross-event by raising the Son. Until then, there is only what appears to be the final triumph of the way the world usually works in any event: the strong inhumanely crush the weak. Apart from resurrection, there is no reason to think that this supposition has been anything but confirmed.

When Paul claimed to the Corinthians that "we preach Christ crucified," he was not just referring to the content of the preaching, its central topic, or its most important theme (1 Cor 1:23). He was also establishing an important claim about the action of preaching itself—the *way* that the gospel is proclaimed when it is preached authentically. The preaching shares in the powerlessness of the cross; it evinces sheer reliance on promise for its success; it makes no claim for the meaning of the cross apart from the demonstration of God's power that flows from a cross that God has met with a resurrection. The gospel preached, in other words, must be cross-like if it is to be true. Yet for precisely this reason, it is vulnerable to refutation, neglect, and unbelief. Preaching the gospel may always suffer as Jesus did; when it has been made impervious to defeat, it has in fact already defeated itself, falsified its truth and imperiled its witness. Paul's preaching to the Corinthians could even be an alternative to his baptizing them for this very reason (1 Cor 1:17).

In asking whether Christ's suffering brought us salvation by *satisfactio*, Thomas Aquinas avoids what is sometimes called the penal substitution view.[9] What the Son offers to the Father is not a *death*, but, in a sense, a whole human *life*: his loyalty and obedience. There is a background within the Bible's narrative that helps illuminate this. It is thought that the martyrdom accounts, especially in 2 Maccabees and 4 Maccabees, partially furnish the New Testament with some of its language for speaking about the cross. For example, placing an emphasis on the devotion, resolve, and endurance under persecution, 4 Macc 17:21–22 speaks of

---

8. Herbert McCabe, *God Still Matters*, 95.
9. Aquinas, *Summa Theologica*, III.48.2.

these martyrs as "having become, as it were, a ransom for the sin of our nation. And through the blood of those devout ones and their death as an atoning sacrifice, divine Providence preserved Israel that previously had been mistreated" (NRSV). Their obedience and faithfulness was greater than that of their nation. Giving their lives in the place of Israel's more widespread disobedience and lack of endurance may, in this sense, be thought of as *satisfactio*. The suffering of the martyrs is vicarious for all of Israel, paralleling the way that Israel's election from among the nations is vicarious—all the world is to be blessed through her.

Likewise, then, with Jesus' own messianic mission and understanding. Israel's long history comes to a head in his life and death; the tragedies of exile, loss, sin, and death are finally dealt with in God's redeeming acts through him. His death not only reveals and discloses the extent of human sin through his killers, but also the extremity of the Son's devotion to the way of God. Moreover, Thomas argues, these two things are not carefully balanced against each other. "Christ's love was greater than his slayers' malice."[10] Only in this sense might we come to call it good news. God's grace in Christ's obedience to the cross brings "superabundant *satisfactio*" by surpassing an exchange in which what is offered (obedience, loyalty, and the experience of exile and death through sin) is in exact proportion to what is taken away. Related to this insight will be that there is more to Christ's resurrection than the strict reversal of the death, which, if it were merely this, we would more accurately describe as *resuscitation*. But only in being *more than* the inverse of death can the life of the risen one be said to *overcome* death. Commenting on Thomas's treatment of *satisfactio*, Frederick Christian Bauerschmidt summarizes that "here the death of Jesus appears to be the result of a sinful human action, which is redemptive only because Christ's love is greater than the hatred of those who killed him."[11] For reasons that will become clear later, I am going to postpone a fuller account of what makes the cross good news, in contradiction to the obvious. Not until we are in a position to speak about the resurrection will what is praiseworthy about Jesus going to the cross be altogether evident.

10. Ibid., III.48.2, reply to objection 2.

11. Bauerschmidt, *Holy Teaching*, 243 n. 11. It is for this reason that untold Christian martyrs have been able to love their killers, but the force of Bauerschmidt's "only" in this comment seems to place the emphasis on the fact that it is *Christ* whose greater love of enemies is redemptive. Those who follow Christ in this manner of dying no doubt pass on a blessing to their killers in a derivative way. I am grateful to Jason Fout for insight on this point.

For now, let us reverse our earlier question about Christ's obedience. Could God really be deserving of our thanks and gratitude if God, acting in Christ for sinners, acts out of necessity? St. Anselm asked, "How shall we attribute our salvation to his grace, if he saves us from necessity?"[12] Anselm answers that what we have been calling necessity ought really to be called grace since God is not being unwillingly subjected to the wills of others (the Son *willingly* accepts the will of the Father to suffer malicious human willing). He freely subordinates himself to the goal of benefiting humanity in its sinful condition. We may be thankful for acts freely undertaken. Anselm maintains further that were there an aspect in which God is held to a prior constraint, it is to God's own (prior) promises. If you make a promise for the benefit of someone else and then act to fulfill it, "the recipient of your favor is as much indebted for your precious gift as if you had not promised it, for you were not obliged to make yourself his debtor before the time of giving [the promise]."[13]

Anselm understands God in Christ as binding himself to promises he made willingly and freely for the sake of humanity. God is thus faithful to his eternal decision to be a savior; there are some things that are "necessary" in order to achieve this—to actualize salvation—and none of these is placed upon God from the outside. They only arise out of God's constancy and integrity, his eternal determination to be nothing other than one who acts in faithfulness to the kind of God that wayward humanity needs. Nor was even the human predicament sprung on God; it did not back God into a corner from which God was unprepared in advance to free himself. "For what man was about to do was not hidden from God at his creation; and yet by freely creating man, God as it were bound himself to complete the good which he had begun."[14] The freedom of God goes back, that is to say, "beyond" the divine decision to create anything whatsoever, without countenancing a compulsion that only arose after the desperate human circumstance became evident. Anselm concludes: "In fine, God does nothing by necessity, since he is not compelled or restrained in anything."[15] And much of what we call *necessity* we really ought to call *grace*.

---

12. Anselm, *Cur Deus Homo*, ch. V, in *St. Anselm: Basic Writings*, 243.
13. Ibid.
14. Ibid., 244.
15. Ibid.

Still, perhaps this discussion about necessity does not solve all of the difficulties surrounding Jesus' suffering. One thing it does not clarify, as shifting the focus immediately reveals, is just *how* the suffering of Christ helps bring about eternal life for those who believe. Again, as I discuss in a later chapter, this latter question is best discussed under the motif of the resurrection. Presently, however, what can be said about God's "definite plan" that is the subject of Peter's preaching on Pentecost? Was there, as many Christians assume, an elaborate plan on God's part to get Jesus killed? Had the Father conspired from all eternity, or perhaps since the fall of Adam, to rescue men and women by the sacrifice of the Son? I suggest that God's plan, fulfilled in Christ being delivered up, is akin to Joseph's reply to his brothers—"you meant evil against me; but God meant it for good" (Gen 50:20). It is the decisive pronouncement on the preceding history. God had not "sacrificed" Joseph, using Joseph's brothers' malicious act of betrayal to do what needed doing as though they were mere tools in his hands. Rather God acted in faithfulness to the covenant made to Joseph's forebears, not only to come to Joseph's aid, but to accomplish more good for him (and his descendants) than he had been made to suffer.

Now, how much does this help answer our question? Who is the agent here? Does this imply that God *means* evil only to act so as to make it in fact mean good? No. As with Christ's suffering and death, we are dealing, as Thomas says, with necessity of the end proposed: a tragic set of events that God does not allow finally to succeed against the divine will. When God rewrites the end of the narrative, tragedy becomes comedy in the newly revealed way that we are given to speak about what only looked to be headed toward inexorable denouement.

We might get the impression from all of this that Jesus only exercised his freedom toward obedience in the face of political opposition. Certainly the political factors are important to understanding what the death of Jesus "means" since, most straightforwardly, the New Testament portrays Jesus as the victim of political and religious opposition and intrigue. (John's Gospel goes out of its way to implicate "the Jews" more than the Romans; Matthew does the same thing by other means [Matt 27:25]. When we talk about "political" reasons for Jesus' execution, we should not imagine that we are excluding "religious" ones.)

Free in Death

I have been considering here the manner of Christ's freedom, specifically to go to the cross, or at least not to avoid going to it, which in the end amounts to the same thing. We are led into thinking about the humanity of Jesus. The way in which Christ is free surely tells us something about how we are free if, as Christianity has traditionally claimed, Christ is one with us in our human nature. Having looked at how the idea of necessity, when inadequately understood as a kind of divine compulsion, threatens the freedom of Jesus in his mission, let us consider another form of limitation—that of being human—that is more difficult to grasp since it is also a way in to speaking about the most genuine way of expressing and inhabiting freedom.

> It is because to be myself is to live the life of a real person, Jesus Christ, that Christianity is concerned with both freedom and limitation. If I break those limits which constitute the humanity of Christ, I cease to be myself—I become unspontaneous, an actor playing an inauthentic role. To sin is therefore to undo myself, to fall into nothingness, into the kind of limitless freedom which ... [is] absurdity, bound up with an immature inability to become a person. To sin is to refuse the freedom to become a particular person for the freedom to be everything and therefore nothing. The social correlative is the vagrant .... [16]

The freedom of Jesus Christ is not the absolute, unlimited freedom so prized by vagrant modernists for whom the untrammeled will floats around in disdain of every closure. Christ's freedom is merely human freedom—the freedom of a man that includes within itself the limits appropriate to being human. Among such limits are physicality, language, death, locality and spatiality, temporality, relational attachments to some and not others, love that both binds us to some others and makes us available to them. These are all limitations that come with what it means that in being one particular person you close off all other particular identities. Jesus Christ was just so also limited (he is, for example, still a Jew).

The modern spirit famously rebels most strongly against this kind of closure, insisting that all options be kept open, that every route constantly remain available to changing whims and altered life plans.[17] It is, anyway, a

---

16. From Eagleton, *New Left Church*, 163.

17. An extreme form of this characteristically modern rebellion can be seen in how young people are educated, especially in the United States. The assumption, now exceedingly common, that college education is a basic requirement for living betrays the

Christian skill that is surely difficult to learn under any circumstances and especially so when there are considerable pressures to unlimit one's sense of who one ultimately is. The fear of commitment so readily diagnosed by psychotherapists (especially of the armchair variety) turns out to be a thoroughgoing enchantment in the contemporary world with promises so ultimately empty that what looks like their fulfillment is really just other promises reissued. If Herbert McCabe is right that Christ's life is the only fully human life, then it is one whose particularity is not finally at odds with his spontaneity; his freedom to be himself is not something at odds with his *actually* being himself; his being something specific (as incarnation implies) is not a merely truncated version of a more determined attempt on his part to be everything. "Jesus died of being human. More than that: all humans die, but he was so human he had to be killed."[18] Christ's exercise of freedom is nothing other than an ultimately human freedom in its being more fundamental than a range of choices that can be measured by potentiality. To speak of Christ's freedom as One raised by the Father, therefore, is only to emphasize how one inhabits the story of one's life and is only as such one's self.

Jesus may surprise because he is living. But he will be limited and constrained, in a sense, by his faithfulness to his own story since the life that he is now living is still a human one, is continuous; Jesus has never stopped being incarnate. A certain postmodern fascination with discontinuities as an antidote to heavy-handed identity-making blazes the culture it creates with continuous discontinuity and randomness. But that ideology is easier to state than the culture is to live. Even the most earnest postmodernist hopes the payroll department will hold itself to enough continuities to get the paychecks out at regular intervals.[19] Predictably

---

fundamental American disdain of hierarchy, especially of educational elites. The more people receive higher education, the less chance there will be for an elite class to claim their uniqueness. Yet the tensions that arise between a meritocracy (higher education) and a social philosophy of sheer egalitarianism in which each citizen is forever perched equidistant from the goods otherwise sought and merited are undeniable. It is not possible to hold open the dream of a flat society while also positioning it before a set of economic and other goods whose very desirability depends on their unequal distribution. Scarcity often breeds desire. The tension, however, is a very real correlative of the mythic freedom I have been discussing in which closure, rather than simply being understood as a feature of our identity as particular humans, is instead seen to be an enemy and impediment of a fully flourishing human life.

18. McCabe, *God Still Matters*, 96.

19. I believe this example comes from Terry Eagleton, although I cannot find it.

enough, the actual effect of an ideology (or anti-ideology) of discontinuity is to produce a numb people who are insensitive to greater and greater stimuli. It is not only difficult to get a reaction out of a people who have been discouraged from looking for connections between things, but even their non-reaction may be construed to them as evidence that the connections do not exist. In many ways, the postmodern distrust of metanarratives has backfired.

Hegel adduced that absolute freedom *necessarily* lacks content as it, in being absolute, rebuffs all restraints. But then, as Eagleton remarks, "absolute freedom spells the death of difference" since it can never find itself reflected in the particulars over which it runs.[20] It is not as though individuals cannot be free according to this doctrine, but they must do so by simultaneously affirming and denying the same things. The modern individual is notoriously one who is *autonomous* (literally, a law unto oneself), which is to say unbounded, dissociated from all others. But at the same time, this autonomy becomes a liability in direct proportion to its success in declaring and situating itself as such. To be free in this sense is to be profoundly particular (which is always unavoidable even when it goes unacknowledged) while remaining unmarked by any particular characteristics. It is to be uncommitted through allegiance, history, and tradition but still unable to do away with the very thing that stubbornly seems to hang around—one's self. The modern move toward emancipation from self-incurred tutelage (in Immanuel Kant's famous formulation) therefore leads to the ideal emancipatory event as death itself, the evacuation of the very self who paradoxically seeks to be free. There is as a result nothing in *life* in which a self can be free so long as to be free is ultimately to be free *from life itself*. Practically, we are dealing with a self that is perennially pressing in the direction of the *generic*: the hollowed out, the blanc. Perhaps intentionally, it is a self that is very difficult to place politically and so is certainly politically impotent. This is partly due to the fact that a self-determining agent for a particular sort of social and political life—understood as what it means to live a free life—cuts against the modernist utopian vision. The denizens of a postmodern-styled micropolitics claim to have discovered alternative forms of power to what sovereigns traditionally wield in plain sight and usually to great effect. But it is worth asking how much the micropolitical exhibits a shrinking

20. Eagleton, *Holy Terror*, 75f.

or even disappearing social vision in the name of an idealized freedom whose end is the extinction of the political animal.

If Eagleton is right that absolute freedom is the enemy of difference, then the freedom that Christianity posits—as freedom for self-determination in proportion to obedience and freedom in God—spells liberation of particulars. Christ's freedom is radically unmodern in its tenacious attachments, its unwavering fidelity, and its resolute constancy. He does not stand in opposition to self-expression since his own expression as himself the irreducibly particular communication of the divine self is the ground of any other authentic particular expression, including mine and yours. This, then, is an utterly genuine and sanguine Christian universality—a connection of particulars in which difference, rather than being excluded, is brought within the complex story of the Messiah of God. And rather than being characterized by severing, disconnection, and association, leaving estranged individual lives and histories that are more free the closer they resemble death, the christological reality instead is characterized by incorporation and redemption. The astounding freedom of Christ, therefore, lies in our ability at the same time to confess his limitations as partly constitutive of what it means for him to be free, rather than to admit shamefacedly that he, like ourselves, is less free for having them.

Christ's freedom is thus a consummately human freedom. He could not have been more free without being less human. And this is in no way a difficulty unless one assumes that the human problem and dilemma flows from our being limited in these ways. Instead, Christianity has not generally thought that our problem lies with our being human but with our being sinners. To be human is to share in a creaturely status that God has deemed "very good" (Gen 1:31). The fall did nothing to affect this. If it had, then Christ's humanity would need to be subjugated in face of his divinity; it would need to be overcome in order for Jesus to be faithful to the will of the Father. Yet this is decidedly *not* what the church worked out when it insisted on Christ having two natures, one human and one divine, yet both of them "fully" his. These two natures are not at odds, and certainly not in a way that parallels human enmity with God. Quite the reverse, in fact, and to precisely the reverse effect: Christ's two natures are in perfect harmony and this is the human hope—that this very harmony might be restored between ourselves and God.

Finally, among the forms of Christian universality at odds with modernity's generic attempts at universal things, may be ranked even the sometimes putative non-particular "Word." Christianity adapted its fascination with the word *Word* (*logos*) from pagan thought. "Word" is a particular instance of the universal that it is. "Word" is a word. As such, it can be said to mediate its own specific existence from within a universal class (in this case, of other words). It is proof positive that the class it denotes is not just an abstraction within which we conveniently put a variety of specific kinds—think *category* or *genus*, like how we talk about languages or currency or pasta. Word is denoted, rather, *by the same existence* of a particular incarnation of it. What is more, since it is impossible to imagine that there could be words without having a word to talk about it, the particularity of "Word" logically precedes and is more fundamental existentially than the class of things (words) to which it belongs. It is instructive to think about Christ in this precise sense: his uniqueness is absolute since it does not follow from, say, ideas about what messiahs are generally like, as though Jesus were merely very rare or very different. He is utterly particular, and, in respect of his humanity, the Christian may share in his real human life and the freedom entailed by his uniqueness—all without a hint of contradiction.

I have been arguing from several angles that the manner of Christ's freedom is in respect of his humanity and in his capacity for obedience and submission to the Father. He undergoes a specific mission that involves his death through the free choice of being faithful to God's way. Yet Christ is also unique in his identity as the Messiah of God, exemplified by how he is the "Word" of God. In both cases—in the humanity he shares with us as well as in his office as Messiah that he does not share with us—Jesus is free from external compulsion. As free, his life is full of surprises for us.

chapter five

Jesus Christ in the Present Tense

So far, I have been dealing with what I take to be extremely surprising things: that God became a man in Jesus Christ, for example. But I am also aware that Christians have perhaps long ago got over being surprised by them. Have we failed to account for their astounding incongruence with the normal course of human affairs by allowing them to become too familiar to us? Have the mysteries simply stopped being mysterious? Have we domesticated their wildness, incorporating them within known spaces, relating them to things more readily grasped? Have we grown impatient in waiting for more or even merely lost the desire? I have been determined in this book to think through what has been lost along the way.

It seems to me that, in looking to the resurrection, we encounter something of this complexity that, in this chapter, I want to wade through. In particular, how can God's promise of Christ's resurrection be freed to be something that continues to be unknown, unexpected, and unresolved and so elicit an enduring, commensurate faith? That the risen Christ lives and so continues to issue the call "follow me" means that he always presently walks forward into an unexpected future that cannot be delivered ahead of time without undoing the call to follow. What, in short, is the danger in over-expecting the resurrection?

I am aware that I am treating the resurrection of Jesus in continuity with discipleship. I am also aware that this is not always done, particularly when the exalted Son of God is separated from the human life of Jesus of Nazareth (or when the former yields theology—Christology and the doctrine of God—and the latter yields history). But I think it is crucial to unite the two since the exalted Christ who is seated at the right hand of the Father is the one who presently lives the risen life of Jesus; the eternal Son of God is, in his eternity, living forward the very temporal existence that structured his life in the Eastern Mediterranean in the first century. Christ has not been removed from history into a timeless eternity; his is still a timeful life, which means, at the very least, that we are not entitled to a settled knowledge of who Jesus is. And this will certainly not be granted to us by his resurrection without undoing itself.¹

Nevertheless, isn't it right to say that the resurrection itself shows us God? This is a question that calls to mind some of the same dialectics that we encountered in the incarnation. If the gospel of Jesus Christ is one of "opening the windows" or of proclaiming from the housetops the secrets of a formerly esoteric knowledge (Matt 10:27), does not God's darkness promise, and indeed threaten, to break like the dawn over every dark night, uncovering "what has been hidden from the foundation of the world" (Matt 13:35)?² Yet surely these dialectics only serve to put a finer point on these matters, for it cannot be that the unexpected, in the sense that I have been discussing it here, intends the same thing as *secrecy*, that some know something that ought to be hidden from others, that there is anymore anything at stake in covering up Jesus' true identity. This is evident enough from the Gospels themselves in the so-called messianic secret when Jesus sternly warns his followers not to disclose to others his true identity as Israel's Messiah (e.g., Mark 8:27–30). After the cross and resurrection, however, the women at the tomb are not silent out of obedience but out of fear (16:8), having explicitly been told to "go, tell" (16:7). It seems reasonable, then, that "Messiah" only receives its complete narrative meaning *after* Jesus is raised.

1. My debt to the theology of Robert Jenson will be particularly evident throughout this chapter even though I do not acknowledge the specific debts at every point. That God is known only through contingent events in time, that the resurrection definitionally identifies God with itself in time as the final event of the story of God's identity, and related defenses of God's timefulness are worked out in Jenson, *Systematic Theology*, vol. 1.

2. I deliberately borrow the famous phrase "opening the windows" from Pope John XXIII who applied it to the church and its need for Vatican II reforms in order to respond to a changing world. There is a considerable note of irony, however, in reforms that many consider—rightly, in my view—as having the effect of bringing the world into the church more than the reverse, and this as at least a correlate of fading mysteries.

83

Framing the question as a properly theological one, we are asking about the nature of revealed knowledge. On the one hand, it is tempting to think that knowledge of God and the things of God—once revealed to the human mind and senses—become just like everything else that we know, subject to both recall and forgetting, but nevertheless at our immediate disposal. However, this clearly severs the continuing presence of God from the knowledge God imparts, detaching facts about God from the divine promise to inhabit them as their continuing truth, sundering information from faithfulness to it—both God's and ours. Saint Augustine asked to know which comes first: calling on God in faith or knowing him. Why the confusion? Because seeking God is already an act of believing in God: "But who calls upon you when he does not know you?" And yet "surely you may be called upon in prayer that you may be known."[3] Knowing does not kill prayer. It does not suppress the seeking. The other temptation is simply the opposite one. It is to underplay the fact of God's self-revelation, principally through Christ, and perhaps to suppose that we have been left in a sweet postmodern darkness to find numbing comfort in a night in which every cat is grey.

The first temptation gains knowledge but strips God away in the process. The second temptation is only too happy to think that the way to hold onto God is to let go of how he reveals himself. Both are beset by a similar irony: the first prefers knowledge of God to God himself and finds too much comfort in what is known; the second prefers a lack of knowledge to God himself and finds too much comfort in the unknown. The dialectics therefore do not unwind or resolve themselves into either of these two unacceptable poles. Instead, they only clarify that when mystery encounters a fervent hope, neither the mystery nor the hope disappears. God is, as St. Augustine wrote, "deeply hidden yet most intimately present."[4]

As modern people, we should admit just how difficult this is to conceive since we have been taught that desire and hope are the enemies of knowledge. But not so for a great deal of Christian thought for which hope is transformed when it encounters God in time. Hope delights in the discovery that its waiting is over only to be renewed by a more profound desire for more, the arrival of which, paradoxically, asks us to wait. This is the opposite of hope being so satisfied that its object is converted into something now possessed. Rather, hope's desire is deepened and

3. Augustine, *Confessions*, I.1.
4. Ibid., I.4.

Jesus Christ in the Present Tense

awaits more. Its unexpectation learns to expect further, exceeding itself in one desire filled with the unanticipated longing for another, more ardent one. As mysteries are "made known," in other words, they transmute into further hopes, questions, and desires that neither satisfy as mere objects of knowledge nor stifle the unknowing desire that came before. This means, crucially, that even when humanity knows God face to face and addresses him unmediated in eternal singing, hope will not have come to an end—in fact, our hope will continually be met and deepened, turning and rolling upward into God. For precisely this reason, the faithful will never tire of their singing.[5]

The desire we most naturally associate with this kind of longing, waiting, meeting, having, and un-having is love. The intimacy that love names requires enough distancing that it not collapse into self-love. But it also has its own rhythms of collapsing and separating since we do not properly call love those things that, in becoming "one" with each other, actually dissolve into patent identity. And it is not only a spatial nonidentity that love requires ("love making" depends on the body's boundaries in order to cross them). Love is also temporal in exactly the sense that I have been describing here as the time of the risen Christ. Desire and fulfillment of desire form an undulating temporal rhythm that would cease to be love if it should flatline as either one or the other, eternally unmet desire or eternal fulfillment, wholly unknown or wholly known.

The human desire to know is a profound desire. So let's go back now and ask how Christians ought to know Jesus as the one raised by the Father. Using the same term he used when discussing the incarnation, St. Thomas Aquinas argued that the resurrection was "fitting" (*conveniens*), indeed that it behooved Jesus to rise from the dead.[6] Even though the cross saves us, the resurrected life of Jesus perfects us in the good by bestowing and returning to the faithful—indeed to all of creation—the incorruptible humanity of the Son of God and thereby ensuring God's perfect and unmediated fellowship with his creation. In some Christian circles, especially ones given to apologetics in a juridical mode, there is often a great deal of anxiety about the resurrection of Jesus as a historical event. Like all historical events, we must surely deal with the resurrection

---

5. This suggests, I think, that the enemy of desire and hope is boredom. Or perhaps better: the problem of boredom is not in lack of desire but in being too easily satisfied by neglecting and ignoring the deeper desires.

6. Aquinas, *Summa Theologica*, III.53.1.

as a contingent fact and Christian claims that the resurrection happened as claims about contingent facts of history, which is to say, facts that might have been otherwise. Such facts need not necessarily be thought of as random in the sense that, in retrospect, any one occurrence will make as little sense as any other.

The key for Thomas, however, is considering these things in retrospect, and this is what distinguishes *conveniens* from proof. The fittingness or suitability of something like the incarnation or the resurrection is a judgment of reason, but it is not one that can be exercised ahead of being confronted by it. It is a skill of making sense of all the disparate elements that, when encountered in real time—in the present tense—defy explanation and only elicit whatever existential response that is most appropriate. If Christians have become accustomed to speaking of the incarnation and resurrection of Christ, it cannot be because they expected them to happen: the prophets, after all, were largely ignored. It must be because, through their ritual and other encounters with the risen Christ in worship, prayer, and the language of liturgy and the Scriptures, Christians have been schooled in the gospel's diction, its proper descriptive discourse, its modes of naming and portraying facts and events after the fact as precisely "fitting"—even, and especially, those things that are accommodated with human living only with difficulty and, even then, awkwardly and while generating a great many questions. *Lex orandi, lex credendi*.[7]

This is all the work of the church's continuing life together. And it is not only the work of theologians that touches it or that seeks to make sense of God's acts after the fact. It is, in fact, primarily the work of the church's complex way of learning to inhabit the ways it has been taught to speak. This surely takes time, practice, and discipline, just as it also requires trust in order to continue speaking things that we believe but cannot fully claim to know. "Fitting" can be misleading, then, since it will not all fit together until God is all in all and we cease being troubled by questions for which the immediate and eternally joyful presence of God is the only real answer.

Nevertheless, it is fitting, as Thomas says, that Jesus was raised from the dead. But he does not attempt to prove that it happened.[8] The desire

---

7. This Latin dictum relates how Christians worship to how they ought to believe and live. It is translated "The law of prayer; the law of belief" and, more loosely, "As we worship, so we will live."

8. In this, Thomas follows Jesus' words to the disciples who had gathered after his resurrection concerning the way that his suffering and death "fulfills" the law of Moses

to prove it through vigorous defense and syllogistic precision risks distorting the very essence of the resurrection itself. It also risks reducing the resurrection to a proof-event of something else such as the reliability of Scripture. John Webster's indictment of evangelical theology along these lines, therefore, is a broader judgment on modern knowing:

> Contemporary evangelical historians of Jesus and his early followers are certainly more sophisticated than their forbears, and a good deal more relaxed about the need to defend the viability of confessional orthodoxy or the reliability and authority of the apostolic witness. What they have in common with earlier work is the fact that their arguments are historical, not theological, and direct themselves primarily to historical reason rather than the judgment of faith. In this sense, they continue the evangelical tradition of Christology "from below"—not in the sense of proposing a "low" Christology, but in treating Jesus and his human history as apprehensible in relative independence from the dogmatic question of his relation to the divine Logos. . . . Jesus' humanity is not graspable as an historical entity without immediate reference to the Word who assumes it; incarnate humanity is not straightforwardly transparent to historical inquiry.[9]

Webster notes the effect this has on the way that the resurrection functions. It is enlisted as part of a set of historical demonstrations that concern themselves with fundamental theology—authority, reliability, truth claims, and so on—rather than the material content of the doctrine of Christ. When this happens, Webster observes, "the resurrection becomes faith's ground rather than its object, and its content has more to do with Jesus's resurrection as past event than with his presence and activity as the risen one."[10] Jesus' resurrection, in other words, is transformed into a "meta" event, one that justifies and verifies something other than itself: it proves that Jesus was killed unjustly and it exonerates his claims to and

---

and the prophets (Luke 24:46). It seems to me that the skill of recognizing something as fitting, while also not robbing it of surprise, is a delicate one and something easily destroyed by an overreliance on the logic of "as it is written." Or, put differently, the ability to cite what was written as part of the story that includes a genuinely unexpected event as its climax depends not only on knowing what is written, but on having already been well practiced in finding the written word quite alive in a variety of life's circumstances. That the written word must just so also be found as living to see the resurrection as something already "written" is therefore perhaps obvious.

9. Webster, "Jesus Christ," 57–58.
10. Ibid., 59.

exercise of a new kind of authoritative teaching; and more to Webster's specific critique, its establishment as an actual event ratifies more general claims about the Bible's trustworthiness on historical topics (and therefore, it usually follows in this logic, on moral topics).

If Webster is correct, then, while the resurrection of Jesus seems to be elevated to supreme importance, it is actually demoted and evacuated of its own dogmatic content when it is enlisted in proofs of claims beyond itself. We may also detect in this precise irony a further irony, namely, that attempts of this kind that make use of history in order to respond to those who antagonize Christian claims on their own historical grounds inadvertently concede the priority of the historical. They therefore end up resembling in mirrored images those positions they attempt most ardently to oppose.

It is in this way that thinking about the resurrection risks taking the surprise out of it. If it verifies something we suspected was true all along, then it is not necessary for us, does not add anything to our understanding of God, does not enrich God's presence with humanity in a way that the resurrection actually brings about. If God raising Jesus from the dead merely establishes more firmly his authority to command and declare, then every command and declaration will not only, by definition, be more important than this act, but also such commands and declarations will likewise owe nothing of their material content to it. Nothing moral or doctrinal will flow from the resurrection that does not already flow from other sources. There is, however, no a priori requirement that the resurrection hold this kind of promise, that it be this kind of "resource" (though "resource" is problematic too, implying, as it does, that what it yields—what it gives "rise" to, we might say—is better than the living presence of Jesus Christ; it is a Christ who serves theology rather than the reverse). But this is the very challenge for Christian expectation as well as the very reality of confronting a promise that will not bend to a priori calculations and projected yields.

When the resurrection is turned into a doctrinal fount, a proof-event that vindicates other claims that are more fundamental than "God raised Jesus Christ from the dead" (such as "We can know that when we are told that God raised Jesus from the dead that we are being told the truth"), it becomes very difficult for the resurrection to say anything doctrinal, or indeed to say anything new at all. So what is the answer to

Jesus Christ in the Present Tense

our question? How can the resurrection continue to speak something new, continue to *surprise*?

Following Webster, the kind of event that the resurrection is can only be attested to in its fullness by witnesses whose existence owes to the truth of the resurrection. The historical reality that this Christ is God and this resurrected Christ lives by the power of God is best seen with the eyes of faith. And that differs from saying that faith opposes the historical or that it opposes the work of reason. As Joseph Ratzinger writes, there is a complex christological hermeneutic here that "presupposes a prior act of faith. It cannot be the conclusion of a purely historical method. But this act of faith bears within itself—historical reason—and so makes it possible to see the internal unity of Scripture."[11] History is at the service of theology's faith as it seeks understanding; but it neither grounds that faith nor is it exercised for its own sake. Put starkly, the fact that Jesus existed at all, or that he lived in Nazareth, or that he ate with sinners is no less interesting historically than that he walked on water or that God raised him from the dead.

Historical work of this sort—whether it intends to discredit Christian claims or to bolster them—is often the attempt to do without the testimony of witnesses. That the historical Jesus is thus the object of the faith of those who believe the ones who speak as his witnesses does not make it any less historical. Still, it is not at all clear what anybody would say or could say about it if it did not produce witnesses. As it turns out, every event shares something of this logic as well. Nothing that happens will be remembered or known as such apart from the existence and persistence of those who bear testimony about it. There is no un-personal (or, as we would normally say, *impersonal*—which is to say *objective*) history to tell about anything since "telling" is precisely the work of people. One need only recall that the resurrection of Jesus was only originally spoken about by those who believed it. Their believing it, like our own, does not *make* it true. But the belief that it is true will not allow those whose belief it is to escape the reality of the event since, if it is true, it will only be known through people who continue to speak about it as such.

We can make the same point differently and by way of conclusion. For Christians, the testimony of the Bible, together with the church's testimony in its worship of Christ as risen lord, is neither just a testament of faith nor merely the remnant of an event otherwise lost to the amnesia of

11. Ratzinger, *Jesus of Nazareth*, xix.

history. Instead, that testimony is simply the only and sufficient witness to the event and, as such, is not somehow able to be discarded should the "event itself" be found with greater purity. There is no event without the witness to it, and this is surely a mysterious kind of knowledge.

It is important to acknowledge how very far all of this is from *proof*, the kind of knowing things that has preoccupied moderns in particular and, not coincidentally, has tended to unite and confuse compulsion (and even violence) with truth. If Christians have ever longed for the message they bear to yield airtight conclusions in their hearers, yearning to be closer to the sciences, they not only cheat the gospel out of its crucial elements of surprise; more significantly, in some respects, this strategy undoes the moral significance of the church as a witnessing body. A gospel whose elements contain their own persuasiveness owing to their inner logic, or to the ability to make demonstrations on historical grounds, unwittingly, perhaps, excludes the way that the church is called by God to bring the truth of the gospel within itself to those who hear it. There is to be no outpacing of the truth Christians proclaim by the ability of that truth to stand on its own. What does this have to do with violence? Violence does the work and takes the place of the persuasiveness of the truth speaking for itself. When our enemies obstinately continue in all manner of unbelief, refusing to come over to our way of seeing things, we may reach for the force of coercion to do what our truth presumably is failing to accomplish on its own.

The modern (and postmodern) inverse of this only restates the way that the association of truth with violence is taken for granted. If the most dangerous people are those who claim to know the truth, then surely the hope of peace lies in admitting that no one is actually in the position to do this. But here "knows" means something quite specific to the modern mind. It is united with compulsion only when it is assumed that internal to the idea of something being true is the entailment that others must believe it on grounds of their shared reason with us. I might write off their disagreement as proof positive of their irrationality, as confirmation that they are in fact the savage beasts that I took them to be all along. Indeed, to posit an alternative to this line of reasoning has long been seen to be a move that beats a hurried retreat into the safety of faith. Famously, faith not only shows itself to be the antithesis of reason, but must necessarily be its enemy.

Nevertheless, stating the problem this way gets things backward. Common reason was originally the great flattener, able to be appealed to in order to settle disputes between warring parties who could not agree on what is true. And since there is only one truth (it is objective), truth was an ally of peace. Yet objective truth came to be the enemy of peace once it was realized how much war and other violence is able to be accommodated within the justifications reason makes for itself and on behalf of itself. But then we might expect that, if faith has already been opposed to reason in this debate, that faith (and subjectivity) would emerge as peace's strongest ally.[12]

There is much that could be said on this topic. At least one thing to notice is that the witness that the Bible is to the resurrection of Jesus is not merely a "text" witness. It is not just the written record of an event nor even just the written record of a testimony of the event. Instead, as intimated above, its testimony is of a piece with the church's tradition, and it is so in two ways.

First, the historical developments that led Christians to recognize Jesus as Lord were not primarily based on their coming to be convinced that the resurrection happened.[13] Christians did not conclude that Jesus had risen from the dead and then worship him as Lord. Instead—and this is already within the New Testament as in Paul's conversion—they found themselves so enmeshed in a way of life and ritual worship that included Christ's continued presence to the church, especially sacramentally, that their way of speaking of Jesus required them to speak about him in the present tense. As they began to speak of the resurrection as a past event, then, their doing so was already conditioned by their sacramental affirmation of Christ's presence.[14] Not only is Paul's conversion as an encounter

---

12. Something of this sort accounts for the reduced objectivity of the scientific enterprise we have witnessed in recent years. Yet the most striking development in this regard must be scientific discoveries that themselves call into question the purported objectivity of science's earlier generations.

13. See the pioneering work by Hurtado, particularly *Lord Jesus Christ*.

14. Could it be that traditions that have gone to great lengths to deny Christ's sacramental presence find themselves needing to "make use of" the resurrection quite differently—as an apologetic device? This was my own experience of the apologetics produced by American evangelicalism in the 1970s and 1980s. For more, see Hovey, "Christian Ethics as Good News."

with the risen Christ an obvious example of this, but so are the ways that the New Testament presents resurrection appearances such as those to Thomas and the Emmaus disciples. In these cases, the risen Christ is in fact a kind of witness to himself. He is only "convincing" that he has been raised by the Father on account of his own presence. That the church's Scriptures contain these stories is not so much a way of re-presenting Christ to us as raised (since we are surely not *ourselves* in these stories confronted with the risen Christ as the characters in the stories were). It is rather a way of presenting us with the testimony of those who were themselves so confronted. The ability for the church, therefore, to affirm that here we also have true testimony about the resurrection depends on the second respect in which these testimonies (the Bible and the tradition) are united.

The second way, then, is the very recognition that *these are our Scriptures* is itself a part of the church's tradition. There is nothing particularly compelling about the witnesses of the resurrection; no reason, especially, why the women at the empty tomb ought to be believed (since in that patriarchal culture, their witness would not have been legally credible). Nevertheless, the church affirms the trustworthiness of their witness *because it affirms the Bible as Christian Scripture to be trustworthy*. We believe the women because we believe the Bible. But, by the same token, the Bible preserves their testimony as part of our Scripture because the Christian community (our forebears and *not* you and me) believed them.

Notice too that the debate about whether these writings ought to be counted as Christian Scriptures is a debate that is long since over. And it is striking that it was largely conducted quite apart from having a "doctrine of Scripture," something that became a shibboleth of modern Protestant scholasticism's specialization in manifold forms of prolegomena. The latter preferred, for example, to begin with "meta" questions like "what is revelation?" that it allowed to outpace the content of revelation. On these grounds, it is inconceivable that the testimony of the women who saw the empty tomb ever would have been believed. Yet for all that can and must be said against the search for theological prolegomena that are functional bulwarks for human certitude and clearing the way for theology to be done, we must finally affirm that what stands "before" it all is not a more fundamental doctrine nor a more comprehensive and general way of arranging the necessary starting points. It is quite simply the actual historical presence of the church persisting throughout the ages in continuity of its witness to "these things" partly and significantly as a body whose use of the Bible in worship and in life attests to its normativity in the articulation of Christian doctrine. Put differently, the "prolegomena" to all subsequent doctrine is not itself a doctrine (such as even the truthfulness of Scripture), but an embodied tradition of churchly practice. In this sense, it is precisely like the resurrection itself. But surely this should come as no surprise given that the church exists as the creation of the Spirit of the risen Christ.

It should be clear that there is much more to the miracle of the resurrection of Jesus than both the miracle itself and the wonder we feel in the face of miracles. Even though I have criticized "proof" and "vindication" above, there is a more salutary way to use these terms. We can surely say that the resurrection is both proof that vindication and victory do not come about through ordinary means and is also itself that vindication and victory. This double move evinces a sacramental logic as the resurrection both points to something else (as being proof of it) and is also the irreplaceable subject matter. It is precisely the sacramental that rescues the resurrection's unexpectedness from knowing and every kind of "meta" reasoning. This is preeminently seen regarding violence.

The cross is clearly an act of violence. It is capital punishment carried out through the collaboration (or assertion and willing submission) of sovereign power and a people whose religious convictions proved powerless to resist it. The cross is Jesus' enduring of violence for love and trust. It refuses to meet violence with violence; it is his definitive turning of the other cheek and walking the second mile. But in this, the cross is perhaps less than remarkable. Many have died for refusing to compromise their ideals. The cross is shown for its uniqueness and indeed its "power" (rightly understood) in its utter disconnection from the ability to produce or yield effects. Why else would it be "a stumbling block to Jews and folly to Gentiles" (1 Cor 1:23)? The cross *must* be a total defeat in this sense. On its own, it does not save: it does not hold back evildoers from committing acts of evil; it is powerless in keeping people from being killed unjustly; it has never convinced Caesar that his is an idolatrous self-image and that his followers worship falsely; it makes no proclamation and can point to no goods. But this does not mean that the Christian story has been left to say little else about the cross. The resurrection not only dawns on a new day but illuminates Good Friday. In fact, the new day is one in which even that dark Friday may now be spoken of as "good." The cross *is* good news, but only because the resurrection vindicates its utter barrenness.[15]

There is no doubt a common way of misconstruing—as simple antitheses—the relation between the cross and resurrection. We would say, perhaps, that the crucifixion is anything but good news, that it in fact is humanity's lowest moment, in which its rejection of God is most concentrated and most acute. But the Father acted to raise up the Son, demonstrating the kind of God that Christianity confesses the Lord to be. The Father, then, not only acts in opposition to the human will to end (or prevent) God's reign in favor of the exercise of the grasp of mortals after power, independence, and self-love. But the Father also reveals the divine will to be more than a mere negation or mirror image of what goes awry in human willing.

Robert Jenson notes that the traditional theories of atonement all attempt to specify what is saving in the death. Each one tries to show how something so counterintuitive as humanity's rejection of God's Messiah in fact amounts to God acting to save the very ones who reject him. While there is an appropriate way of speaking of the crucifixion in these terms, Jenson cautions that "such [atonement] doctrines can be true only if the salvific efficacy they discern in the Crucifixion is located there by virtue of the Crucifixion's narrative unity with the Resurrection. The Crucifixion is God's salvific action just in that God overcomes it by the Resurrection."[16] In other words, the cross is not itself the site of the overcoming, but the beginning of what is certain only by promise. The resurrection is the site of the overcoming. Overcoming of what? Of sin and death, the very things that are in fact the reality of the cross, and not only by way of talking about the things that the cross *means*. To be sure, the cross only means sin and death because it is a death that results from sin. And the sin that put Jesus on the cross, however else Christianity has decided to talk about it as belonging to *all of humanity* or even to *me*, is most immediate and obvious through the narratives that the Gospels tell about how Jesus got there—the events of betrayal, abandonment, and scandal; the

---

15. Still, as Walter Brueggemann cautions, the darkness is not done away with completely: "a feel-good, triumphalist, or therapeutic gospel may permit Sunday to obliterate Friday. But in our honest reading of the New Testament, and in our honest liturgic reckoning, the Friday of negativity persists to make its claim" (*Theology of the Old Testament*, 401).

16. Jenson, *Systematic Theology*, 1:182.

reasons that Jesus angered the religious leaders; the anxiety his movement provoked among the Roman and Jewish elites, and so on.

The attempt here made is to do justice, in a short space, to Jenson's caution. What would it mean to hang on to the narrative unity of the crucifixion and resurrection? It cannot simply be that one follows the other in the sequence of events. Instead, it must have to do with each one having significance only with and through the other. For example, if Christ had not been raised, the cross would not be good news for anybody. (It would doubtless be good news for the ones who caused it to happen, the Romans and the Sanhedrin, but this is hardly the news Christians proclaim—which is its opposite.) The resurrection takes something that would, on its own, be unequivocally bad news and re-stories it by changing the ending. As a result, every failure and scandal along the way takes on a new significance in the narrative of which it is now a part. The goodness of the Father's action in raising up the Son throws back over the entire story elements (and meanings and deep significations) that were not there before. Prior to the resurrection, these were merely events in the same tragedy of human existence that existing this way has taught us to expect. History (we had grown accustomed to telling ourselves) is a series of events in which the strong defeat the weak. There is nothing surprising about that. When it happens, it is no longer even interesting. But the expectation that Mary sang about (proleptically) as a certainty—"He has shown strength with his arm, he has scattered the proud in the imagination of their hearts, he has put down the mighty from their thrones, and exalted those of low degree" (Luke 1:51–52)—is now what defines history since it is the reality of how the Father has acted in raising the Son. The cross is not only part of the action that God has reversed but is in fact itself possible through the Son's obedience in not fighting back to secure his own future. Therefore, the cross may be said to be part of God's single action in Christ: his giving the world himself, his refusal to fortify his own life and destiny if it meant punishing those who would call it into question and destroy it, and his re-gifting by the Father precisely to this crucifying world. Astoundingly, not only can we now talk about the cross as good, Augustine even thought it appropriate to cry, "O blessed sin of Adam"!

In saying these things, I am delivering on a postponement made in the previous chapter. Further to the question of what it is about the resurrection that makes the cross good news is the goodness of the consummate event itself: what is good about the Father raising up the Son? At least two things.

First, it overturns the human verdict by vindicating the condemned. Though it increases the likelihood of being slain by those to whom it presents the superlative challenge, the manner of Christ's living is endorsed by the Father to be of such significance that it merits a horizon of divine judgment beyond the justice exercised by rulers and other powers (which themselves always also rule in one way or another).

Second, it takes the place of the Father's just wrath against human creatures for killing the Son. This aspect is so obvious that it is common to overlook it. Yet if the miscarriage of justice—the false witnesses and so on—that sent Jesus to the cross is shown to be just that, then we would expect that the act of vindicating the condemned would summarily enact the true justice on those responsible for condemning him. They would have felt God's just wrath. This would install true justice and reestablish the divinely given order of things. But this is precisely what did *not* happen. God's act to establish justice in this case in which both the Son and the Father are victims (though in different ways) is actually an act of forgiveness. Humanity does *not* suffer God's wrath for the death of the Son; rather, the Son is re-gifted to humanity. This re-giving *is* the act of foregoing what is rightfully God's to do. Therefore it *is* forgiveness and salvation. The resurrection overcomes sin and death by itself being the final act of the human narrative. Crucially, for the perspective I am presenting here, it is not as though the cross and resurrection (together or separately) *mean* or *merit* or *cause* forgiveness and salvation. They are, in their narrative unity, the actual foregoing of punishment for the sin of crucifying Jesus. We killed God and God did not kill us back.

Herein lies the crucial role for any disciple who determines to live a life of surprise. Christianity may embrace crosses because it knows of the resurrection. Jesus' death can now even be spoken of as "good" on account of the promise that the resurrection has made to those who share in it. How else are we to make sense of the joy of martyrs? They are not joyful at the death, but at the surety of the promise of being raised with Christ, having followed him in their dying. Still, to "know" the resurrection is not really to know very much, nor is it to know something in the way that things are usually known. The resurrection *of Jesus* is an event, but the resurrection of Jesus' followers in the manner of Jesus' resurrection is not yet actual for them. It is for them a promise.

This means that those whose devotion to Jesus leads them to crosses are not comforted by the certainty of resurrection on its own. They are instead convinced of God's faithfulness to fulfilling promises. The disciple's world, in other words, is not a mechanistic one that, however else similar to the present age, overturns every unjust act with a just one, overcomes every death with a life, and unwinds every suffering. Instead, it is one to which God is present and in which God is active, holding forth promises and eliciting belief in them (which is only to say trust in him). The Christian yearns for more of God's world, one that will be most authentically lived when lived alongside God. The gospel's scandal is its declaration that this kind of reckless trust in promises is already a possibility of this world. And not only that, but it is in fact the definitive feature of all of creation. Christianity does not defy the created order when its adherents thrust themselves onto the mercy of God's promises. In fact, the Christian finding God in and among creation is itself an outcome of trusting that the promises are true.

chapter six

Jesus the Stranger

Jesus is the ultimate stranger. Not only is he one we would not naturally choose to befriend, to follow, or to adore. But his resurrected life continues to invade ours. He *disturbs* us with his presence and comes against our every move to keep him down in death. One way Christians have found for keeping Jesus at bay is by insisting that he must be *chosen*. Here the image is of a Jesus who is pleading but nevertheless ultimately passive before a selective humanity. He either plays no role in our picking him or else he exists as a benign force behind something that is eminently more decisive: the more important act, faculty, and right of human choice.

One immediately recognizable problem with this is not only that we will not usually choose something that we do not know, lacking any grounds for judging it worthwhile, for example. But our choosing Jesus as a friend cannot depend on a prior understanding of what it means to be friends with Jesus. How could we know what this friendship would hold for us? Friendship names the process of getting to know a friend.

> You are my friends if you do what I command you. No longer do I call you servants, for the servant does not know what his master is doing; but I have called you friends, for all that I have heard from my Father I have made known to you. You did not choose me, but I chose you and appointed you that you should go and bear fruit and that your fruit should abide; so that whatever you ask the Father in my name, he may give it to you. This I command you, to love one another. (John 15:14–17)

What is most striking is that the friendship between Jesus and his disciples depends on his initiative in making the Father known to them. This kind of knowledge is a gift that remains with them so long as the relationship of love and friendship exists both between Jesus and the disciples and among the disciples themselves. Just as Jesus revealing the Father is a gift, so also is his choosing of them to be his friends. The temptation for Christians to believe that they have chosen Jesus stems from both a fundamental unease with the unpredictability of gifts and also with the bond that gift-giving presupposes and indeed creates. The chooser's choice is dependent on the chooser and never vice versa. The friend Jesus must therefore again and again become a stranger in order to preserve the friendship; by *overchoosing* us (his choice is always bigger than ours), he violates the control our choice attempts to establish; through the presence of a stranger-friend, he disturbs the glib detachment our choosing would preserve.

The most subtle and therefore successful modes of Christian unfaithfulness are those that pass most easily for faithful practice and devotion. They are not found in the outright flaunting of an irreligious life nor in spurning the gospel's moral entailments. Rather they are those actions that attempt to control the uncontrollable God that Christians confess to find displayed in the resurrection of Jesus Christ. When such actions are devotion, they betray self-love. When they are worship, they betray hubris. When they are religious works, they betray a preference for technique and industry.

All friendships exist only in practice. It goes without saying that you cannot be someone's friend on paper, as an idea, or in theory. I cannot introduce myself to someone for the first time and divulge that I have been his friend for many years. So what makes a friendship? It is probably true that friendship is not completely reducible to individual acts committed by friends for each other. But surely it is impossible to conceive of any friendship whatsoever that is totally bereft of them. Friends will with a certain amount of frequency renew their relationship with new acts, and they know that what has passed between them in the past can only sustain them for so long. At some point they will devolve into an ill-defined status of ex-friend if friendly gestures cease entirely. The same goes for how Christianity understands what it means to be friends with God in Christ.

One can appreciate why some Christians feel a certain amount of unease with celebrations of the "personal relationship with Jesus" so prioritized by many contemporary churches.[1] At its worst, this description of the kind of relation Jesus makes with sinners functions to exclude the corporate life of the Christian community in that relationship by denying that we only ever come to God through our fellows.

At the same time, the slogan is not wrong to draw attention to the fact that Jesus cannot be said to be "had" apart from anything other than relationship. And it is certainly marked by many of the characteristics that other relationships have (although it certainly also entails a great deal more). It is something that must be constantly maintained and sustained through effort; it requires engaging in the movement of love, joy, obedience, and fellowship that Christians call discipleship; and it calls for unceasingly employed skills for recognizing Christ in the unexpected that will only ever be renewed to the extent that it is practiced. The church's rehearsal of its friendship with Jesus is most acutely enacted in its love of enemies and its welcoming of strangers. Not only do these things prepare Christians to approach Jesus without "choice" just as one does not choose the things one welcomes (they always choose us). But more to the point, human enmity with God has set us as his enemies before we were made his friends. God loved his enemies before we loved ours, meaning that our love of enemies does not only *include* our love for God but starts with it.

While it is certainly the case that Christian thinking has in almost every respect affirmed Jesus' similarity to us—to our humanity, to our experience of temptation—Jesus is nevertheless different. We must be very careful in how we describe this difference, however. He is not fundamentally different *from humanity*, nor is he superhuman or somehow impervious to human frailty. He is different precisely *because* he is a human; he is different *in* his humanity. He does not pander to our desire for rendering predictable our routine engagements, for making the life of faith much like life at the office, for bringing every uncertainty within the close scope of our knowledge. The gospel affirms as much when it declares and proclaims Jesus as the risen one, no longer a corpse whose existence follows known patterns of decay, the scientific and natural course of events for dead flesh, but the living presence of one who may surprise the world—even, and especially, those whose mission it is so to proclaim

---

1. Though the phrase occurs more widely than many might suppose. For example, Pope Benedict XVI uses it in order to describe the limitations of some modern biblical studies projects such as the search for "the historical Jesus" (Ratzinger, *Jesus of Nazareth*, 2:xvi).

it. The early Christians struggled with how to make sense of Jesus' physicality in this respect, especially as one debate centered on whether his body was inherently incorruptible or whether it was merely saved from corruption through being resurrected.

Some argued that in the days between burial and resurrection, there had been no decay. But it is impossible to know whether this should be attributed to the properties of Jesus' body or to the restorative power of the resurrection itself. The controversy was important to Monophysites who cited to their cause what is at least an ambiguity in Athanasius's work *On the Incarnation*.[2] Athanasius taught that it was unfitting that Jesus should ever become ill since he is the one who healed others of their illness. However, then one is perhaps left wondering whether the one who raised Lazarus and Jairus's daughter should himself be subject to death. "Subject to death" is surely no small characteristic of what is involved in being human; Athanasius would surely agree. Yet where does the difficulty lie?

One problem with this line of inquiry is that it attempts to strike a compromise between the human and divine where Jesus may be accorded human flesh, but not finally flesh that is subject to decay like ours is. Jesus overcomes death, it is assumed, by not himself being subject to it in his humanity to begin with. Whenever Christian thought proposed a superhuman Jesus, it has usually done so intending to safeguard his divinity. When Jesus floats several inches above the ground it is usually because those who think of him that way are looking for ways of buffering the transcendent quality of Jesus' person from the world he enters. In such cases, though, incorruptible flesh nearly renders the resurrection as something intrinsic to Jesus' very body so that we must therefore use scare quotes when referring to his "death" since Jesus always already had new life resident within him. Jesus is saved from a real human death by virtue of his special status as the God-man, his body preserved from decomposition because of his body's nature. Notice, though, that the resurrection then becomes logically necessary and redundant. And if so, then the resurrection is simply inevitable, even routine. The good news ceases to be news.

Instead, Jesus' resurrection is the great "but" that follows his death, the extraordinary contradiction of death itself. As Paul writes, "therefore God has highly exalted him" (Phil 2:9). This exaltation proceeds from the utter finality that the cross is for Jesus. It is free and therefore *different*,

---

2. Athanasius, *On the Incarnation*, secs. 21–23.

as it is a gift that in no way is inherent in either Jesus' life or in his death. Crosses do not yield resurrections. Even "God-men" (an idea absurd to Christians for its plurality) do not hold a secret immortality that humans do not, only then to let it loose three days after being killed. Death is final for Jesus just as it is final for us. He is no different in this respect. Put differently, we will not know him to be different apart from the acts of God to and through him. His difference is God surprising us.

We should acknowledge that this seems to be a paradox, or at least that it suggests a great deal of irony. The proclaimed gospel is always foremost good news. But it is not known to be good on account of its verifying for us those things that we already took to be good. It is not solace for those racked with anxiety as they wait for confirmation that they are on the right side. Nor even does knowing it as real vindicate those who had already committed themselves to God's cause. Rather, the gospel opens the world from fear of strangers to the belief that strangers—even enemies—can be loved and welcomed. In doing so, it does not primarily yield a satisfying knowledge but unsettles our satisfactions, so that the welcome of strangers is not a "position" or a "doctrine" but an uncertain and unstable extension of wonder and love with an equally incalculable return. Even the greatest enemy of the faith is well within reach of God's friendship. And, if so, then she is likewise well within the reach of Christian friendship. Christians have been allowed to release the fear that attempts to control the evil that their enemies intend.

Even so, this is not to say that evil may not still triumph in the short run. Because the extension of friendship is inherently vulnerable to establishing or destroying a relationship, there is no way to safeguard the invitation from being abused without compromising its ability to create something that did not exist before. This means that if friendship is reserved only for friends (rather than enemies), it cannot help perpetuating a sameness in which nothing new comes into being. Relations may be rearranged and shifted around, but no new bonds will be generated. Yet this is precisely what *caritas* does: it creates more love from the current love; it cannot be "expressed" without being exercised, shown without being extended, exercised without being enlarged. Enemies prompt the exercise of Christian love for precisely this reason. The real question is not "Who is my enemy?" but "What is the manner of my love?"

Likewise, release from fear does not mean that the Christian extension of friendship and the invitation of welcome will turn every enemy

Jesus the Stranger

into a friend. The uniqueness of Christian love—and so Christian friendship—is in how it continues to extend itself *in spite of* every refusal. The reason for this is that it does not premise its friendship on reciprocity, on the easy return of every gift given. Instead, it continues to give even in the face of no return in confidence that the gifts we give were never "ours" to begin with and, just so, they are inexhaustible, abundant, and forever being created out of nothing.

We are not creators but creatures. We know we did not create the universe or time itself. But the biggest surprise is that neither are we creators of the things that we think we make, the things that it seems we really do form out of nothing. And this extends, I am suggesting, even to friendship with strangers (remembering that we ourselves were strangers to God). Then this can only really be the case if there is *more* to our actions than we can see; that we act always with remainder with respect to what is easily perceived. I give of myself in generosity to a friend or my spouse, but I cannot pretend that in doing so I have made a friendship or a marriage. These things exceed both our actions and our intentions by themselves being the gracious overtures that embody more than the sum of their parts.

Yet even though Christian love is preeminently tested to prove itself as such in its relation with enemies and strangers, it does not share with modern sentiments a disavowal of the expectation of return. As others have noted, the economics of modern gift exchange is premised on the disinterest of both parties: anonymous "charitable" giving to someone I will never need to get to know or else a formal contract designed to limit the obligations of both parties to what is precisely in the contract—when the contract ends, so does the relationship.[3] Against this, however, Christian giving (friendship with enemies and strangers being an example) so invests one in relationships with others that it opens itself up to the possibility and hope of return. True, it gives without condition; and it does not expect anything as part of its original impulse to give in the first place. Its giving is free, abundant, and an overflow of the joy that comes from trust in God's goodness to continue according to his promise. And this is then the exact reason that it also hopes for, even *expects*, a return. The return is understood to be *part of* the goodness of the gift. It is the manner in which the relationship formed by the initial gift is maintained, nurtured,

---

3. See Long and York, "Remembering."

deepened. Reciprocity is not why we give—it is entailed in the fact that our giving is itself also a continuation of gifts received. Put differently, Christian friendship does not expect any new miracles greater than that which has already made us friends of God.

A modern fear of friendship is only a version of its more fundamental fear of manipulation. It is important to note that for manipulation even to be a possibility assumes a continuous set of relations. *Severing*, we might say, is the modern strategy for achieving freedom and is therefore always dependent on what freedom is *from*: from entailments, constraints, and limitation. By contrast, Christian freedom is only realized through *binding*. To the extent that it is bound to the promises of others, Christian freedom makes lives present to one another, generating the free possibility to be friends. It is more free when it is more bound by greater relations. Unable to countenance a freedom whose paramount feature is anything other than severing, modern reasoning has excluded the possibility of friendship. The loneliness of "enlightened" cultures (think gated communities) is therefore not an incidental by-product of some other development; it is exactly the point of enlightened freedom. All of this is a reminder that the exclusion of strangers is not an alternative to a more fundamental desire for friendship; it is, in fact, merely the inverse of friendship's modern exclusion.

What makes Jesus so disarmingly different is the fact that he does not share with us our notions of power. He does not assess importance and unimportance according to the standard measures, nor does he act and cause things to happen according to the usual manner of displaying and exercising influence.

There is admittedly a very strange logic to this. As incarnate, Jesus is "like us" and so it is easy to assume that his dispossession of divine prerogative (Philippians 2), with its clear analogues with respect to power, is another thing that counts for Jesus being human. But surely we must say that Jesus becoming human, in this respect, has the effect of making him as much *unlike* us as like us. His refusal to cash in on the benefits of equality with God is not just straightforwardly an entailment of his humanity but is crucially also an act of obedience and faithfulness—very unlike ours! But becoming unlike us in obedience and faithfulness turns out actually to be one way that Jesus is more human than we are. The model human life is a life of pure obedience.

Jesus the Stranger

This means that Jesus' difference to us owes, in large measure, to his faithfulness and our faithlessness, his sinlessness and our sinfulness. This is why "the world knew him not" (John 1:10). We do not naturally know how to live as fully human the life of creatures in gratitude and trust in our creator. We will resist the dependence this requires and instead assert the independence generated of our fantasies that we are our own creators. Even though Jesus as the eternal Son of God is "begotten, not made," his human life—as much as his divine life—displays a love that, though originally Trinitarian, nevertheless becomes, within creation itself, the love by which creatures may also enjoy God and share in God's very life.

Yet this kind of difference confronts us with a temptation we may too readily embrace: to assume that human differences are merely covers for a more fundamental distinction between the righteous and the unrighteous, the faithful and the unfaithful, those who know God in Christ and those who do not. How are we to navigate this?

Crucial to the account I have been giving is the way that these two kinds of difference go together. Jesus' difference lies in both his perfect obedience to the Father and also in his freedom as risen from the dead. But these are also two things that Jesus' disciples will share in as disciples. The life of discipleship entails the perfecting of human souls, the reorientation of disordered wills toward God's holy ways, and the healing of wounded passions with the fire of divine love. Nevertheless, lest this perfecting aspect of the gospel's work distort the centrality of Christ as its agent (turning the good news into pure therapy), Jesus' otherness as risen and free constantly disrupts any thought of Christian perfection as being a settled state or a destination already reached. That Jesus remains other to his disciples is not a way of denying their struggle to live a sanctified life as one of following; instead, it affirms that the way *to* God and the way *of* God are not in conflict. Nearer to God, we are nearer the mystery—not delivered *from* it, but *into* it.

Even so, it is a mystery over which we possess little power and over which we may exercise no dominion. If we could do so, it would cease to be a mystery and become to us a possession and one more aspect of our world that we bend to our control, that we manipulate to greater efficiency through technology. It is therefore purely an entailment of God's mysterious coming to us in Christ that Christians are confronted with an event before which we become powerless. This does not mean that the gospel is immune to human power, even violence. It is clearly subject to its worst ravages. What it does mean, however, is that such things are enfolded within the very structure of the good news. The gospel is not only good despite human grasping, its godlike attempts to bring everything that is unpredictable within our control; but the fact that it remains a promise to us in the midst of that power difference is the very substance of its goodness.

Jesus' different power finds profound expression in the faces of all excluded people, including children and the poor. It is appropriate that Jesus' embrace of children during his ministry is usually one of the first things that children are taught about him. After all, their coming to know it as true of him is a facet of the welcome that Jesus himself continues to exercise through the church. Welcoming children is more than an interesting fact about a fatherly figure or an endearing feature of a friendly teacher. It is simply one of the many forms that a life naturally takes when it is freed from the usual ways of getting things done. If the world's way reserves success for those who are already successful, and power for those who are already powerful, it ensures this nepotism of sorts through good connections, which is simply to say, through "friends" of importance. This is the self-evident story of the world, the reason that the rich grow richer and the poor grow poorer. The route to any kind of recognizable success is through people who wield influence.

What is perhaps most special about Jesus' embrace of children is not what is typically pointed out—that children are especially prized for their innocence. To be sure children are relatively innocent (although some might suspect that innocence is sometimes just a gentler way of referring to ignorance). A child will ask questions, for example, simply because he wants to know the answer. Adults find innumerable reasons to keep from asking about what they do not know: someone has convinced them that it is unimportant or irrelevant, that it is rude or distracting, that we have all grown weary of our inability to come up with satisfactory answers and have stopped asking. The innocence of children is prominent in other respects and probably does explain why they came to Jesus without fear. They came without self-consciously policing their own actions.

Yet there is more to Jesus' clear alacrity to keep company with the little ones. It surely has more to do with their social weakness, their powerlessness to make for adults an achievement out of their friendship. To be "such as these, to be as children, means being insignificant, someone of no value in the eyes of society."[4] Like the rabbi who befriends fishermen, the one who welcomes children welcomes those who are not capable of offering much in return. Jesus describes himself and the Father as the object of this same welcome among those capable also of receiving rejected and seemingly politically and socially useless prophets (Matt 10:40–42). Also, Paul addresses the church in Corinth concerning God's choice of the lowborn, despised, and non-influential (1 Cor 1:26–29).

Then again, their inability to offer much in return is not really a *reason* for befriending children. It is simply the way they are, and attending to them is the way God is.[5] When we join in God's attention to children, it frees those who would otherwise be constrained in their choice of friends. There is a hint of Immanuel Kant's ethic of treating others as ends and never as means. But there is also a great deal more to any friendship than the affirmation of a principle like this one. It is the friendship itself, the powerless embrace of another for the purity of the relationship uninfluenced by considerations of usefulness. When Jesus next teaches his disciples the lesson learned by the rich man who cannot follow Jesus due to his great wealth, Jesus addresses them as "children" (Mark 10:24). The issue is not innocence but the idea that the kingdom of God cannot be bought; it does not repay. So it is most obviously enjoyed by those who, like children (and, we must surely add, *including* children), never even come close to playing that game.

This need not mean that befriending children brings no actual rewards. It is just that the rewards are kept from being extrinsic to the friendship itself. We might think about parallels such as the difference between enjoying something versus treating it as an investment: these two will yield very different accounts of "value" and understandings of what is happening when they are "experienced." Friendship is its own good and is not in service to other goods (not an investment). Most parents already know what this means. People who want to have children *for any reason* not only may be setting themselves up for disappointment. They

---

4. Gutiérrez, "Option for the Poor," 242–43.

5. Jon Sobrino says as much about the poor: "The reason the Reign [of God] is addressed to the poor is simply the way God is. God's being thus, and not otherwise, is neither conceptualized nor conceptualizable . . ." (Sobrino, "Central Position of the Reign of God in Liberation Theology," 370).

are also placing a very great burden on their children to be something particular, to satisfy a predetermined need, to meet an expectation that was formulated in advance of their birth. This constrains children rather than grants them freedom; it construes their very existence as a means to an end for somebody else. To be sure, no child will be utterly free from roles and expectations placed on them by parents, the community, and the church, nor should they be; the hope that we might "keep their options open" shows disdain for the kinds of people we will inevitably (if partly) shape our children into becoming. The difference lies in the kind of un-freedom that comes from enlisting children in adult life and for the benefit of adults. For example, Rowan Williams reflects on how our society teaches children to be consumers:

> We hustle children into pseudo-adult roles and choices as soon as we decently can, or rather sooner than we *decently* can—especially through the systematic assault on the child as possible consumer which is represented by modern advertising of toys and leisure goods. Although this looks like provision for children's needs or wants *as* children, the truth is that it creates habits and expectations that assimilate the child into the most obsessional adult purchaser.[6]

Adult life is impatient with the otherness of children. Rather than being a society that discovers and works with the real needs of children, we have one that seems to know only how to make them into something other than what they are. In many churches, this same impulse requires a child to stop being a child in order to fit the ethos of the congregation. Williams goes on to ask, with Donald Nicholl, "How can you live in accordance with the teaching about being children if you are for ever hiding yourself away from children?" And how can theology be done in and by communities "where men and women are together, and . . . where children are not hidden away"?[7] One answer must be that it will be done in a way that refuses to treat children (or anyone else, for that matter) as means to an end.

If friendship with children is marked by refusals to instrumentalize the relationship, it will be most genuine when freedom is given to the "little ones" as a discipline of *un-expectation*. It is the case that Aristotle thought that friendships of this kind were impossible—when the

---

6. Williams, *Christ on Trial*, 62–63.
7. Cited in ibid., 63.

Jesus the Stranger

relationship is this imbalanced, it is likely that one party will be in the position of wanting to gain from the other. The more different the parties are from each other, the more likely the difference will lead one to exploit something in the other. On the other hand, if there are friendships that exist, in a sense, for their own sake, Aristotle assumed they would have to exist between near equals. Family relations present a strikingly different case since these relations are given and not freely chosen. You do not choose who your uncle is, yet you are bound to him. This does not mean that you cannot be friends with your uncle; only that the crucial obstacle to friendships being able to escape their instrumentalizing tendencies has already been overcome by the mere fact that the relation is a familial one.

This helps explain how brothers and sisters in Christ occupy a new kind of friendship—one that mimics kinship in making possible that they may now be to each other "for their own sake." At the same time, because Christians in most cases will not have a biological kinship with these brothers and sisters, their friends may circumvent Aristotle's worry. This is particularly important, I submit, when it comes to being friends with children, particularly the children of others. (I am more likely to have this "for their own sake" relation with my own children; often for children there are no other such relations, but if so, this is a function of adults not welcoming them as Jesus commanded.)

Incidentally, that Jesus was not a parent to these children indicates something of a program for childless Christians (which clearly includes married people as much as singles). Karl Barth asked, "Is it really true that an involuntarily childless marriage is not a normal and complete marriage?" And if so, "do not all such disqualifications suggest a relapse into an abstract Old Testament mode of thinking? One might have spoken in this way *ante Christum natum*. But what does it really mean to continue to do so without further examination *post Christum natum*?"[8] Christ himself was the last child who *needed* to be born. He decisively and conclusively fulfills the promises to Israel and so is himself Israel's "descendants."[9] God's covenant promise to Abraham has been fulfilled in Christ, overcoming and bringing to an end that strong drive, so palpable in the stories of the Old Testament, to lament barrenness for being a sure sign of God's disfavor.

---

8. Barth, *Church Dogmatics* III.4, 266. I am grateful to Jonathan Tran for helping me see the significance of Barth's argument.

9. Or, as Paul argues in Galatians 3, God's promise to Abraham was to him and his offspring (Christ), not offsprings.

Yet even there, as Barth notes, the curse of barrenness is slowly being undermined. "The unfruitful wife emerges again and again, not only as the embodiment of need and misery and abandonment, but also of the hope of Israel and all the righteous in Israel, of the splendid future in which God will be wonderfully revealed as its Savior."[10]

Barth's argument is striking: there is no need for any other children to be born. Yet it is just as crucial that this does not suffice as a reason not to have children. Only now children are no longer the guarantors of God's faithfulness to the future. They may be free from these anxieties (which have only ever been adult anxieties anyway). It also indicates that because of Jesus, children may be friends who fulfill no external compulsion or requirement. Their presence may be sheer gift, and it is no surprise that Jesus treats them as such. Those without children of their own may likewise welcome the children of others as gifts precisely because they do not "belong" to their parents, do not play a role in the necessary life of the family. Like Jesus, they "belong" to the church. This is a belonging of friendship. We may say that we "have" children in the same sense that we "have" friends—not as possessions but as gracious and free presences. We should suspect, then, that those who have no time for children have no time for true friends, that is, friends who would exist to them for no extrinsic purposes, for no purposes other than friendship.

Still, it would be wide of the mark to conclude that this is a problem shared only by unpleasant and nasty people. In fact, it is one of the chief characteristics of modern existence. The contemporary ethos prizes the conversion of external goods over internal goods or, better, it subtly attempts to convert all internal goods to external ones. Its spirit demands that we justify all of our attachments, and the justifications expressed in terms of their utility are generally the strongest and most convincing. Politically speaking, this is the reason that pubic discourse more readily grasps at rights than at goods. Appealing to goods naturally entails that there will be people you are unable to convince. After all, modernity is premised on the question of how to negotiate a society where we can no longer assume that goods are widely shared. It is a prudent kind of public face that looks for those things that are most widely shared in order to establish consensus.

Much has been made of this aspect of modern existence. I simply want to point out that notions like consensus are themselves goods, only

10. Barth, *Church Dogmatics* III.4, 266.

no one questions whether they rightly help us identify what is worth pursuing. There is nothing inherently insidious about a society persisting in tacit agreement over a good that is positioned at this very high level. However, there is surely something disingenuous about invoking a good as a way of limiting public discussion of goods. What does this have to do with children? Simply this: the impulse that keeps modern people from conceiving of goods as political is precisely the same as the impulse that devalues adult friendship with children. The impulse is expediency; and expediency is the covert modern way of describing the most valued expression of power.

At the same time, children can function for a people as symbols of their destiny and reinforce their belief in the goodness of their culture. For example, *New York Times* columnist David Brooks reflects on a strange but fruitful question: What would happen if a bizarre solar event ended up sterilizing the people on the half of the earth facing the sun at that moment? Brooks surmises that the result would demonstrate that we are not nearly as individualistic as we think since our dependence on culture and community for sustaining us—not to mention the hope of a future world for our posterity, the hope of which we live in the present—makes survival more than an individual concern. In reality, says Brooks, we would surely anticipate deep crises:

> If, say, the Western Hemisphere were sterilized, there would soon be a cataclysmic spiritual crisis. Both Judaism and Christianity are promise-centered faiths. They are based on narratives that lead from Genesis through progressive revelation to a glorious culmination.... Believers' lives have significance because they and their kind are part of this glorious unfolding. Their faith is suffused with expectation and hope. If they were to learn that they were simply a dead end, they would feel that God had forsaken them, that life was without meaning and purpose.[11]

No doubt Brooks is right that global sterilization would present no small spiritual crisis, but I do not think it should, at least not for the reasons he gives. There is something amiss in his description of the centrality of promise for Jews and Christians. After all, the most poignant biblical crisis over the promise's "glorious unfolding," God's covenant promise to Abraham, has precisely to do with sterility, the very possibility of *any*

---

11. Brooks, "Power of Posterity."

descendants for Abraham. This is why Abraham and Sarah both laugh at the idea (Gen 17:17; 18:12). The lesson of Abraham's faith is that the promise is still in effect despite the almost certain knowledge that it is impossible. It *is* impossible on the basis of the present order of things. New life from death re-births hope from the sterile womb.

> By faith Sarah herself received power to conceive, even when she was past the age, since she considered him faithful who had promised. Therefore from one man, and him as good as dead, were born descendants as many as the stars of heaven and as the innumerable grains of sand by the seashore. (Heb 11:11–12)

What Brooks assumes is that Jews and Christians live by a hope that cannot withstand a spiritual crisis, that they are only equipped with and hold onto those promises that seem most likely to be fulfilled. It is true that discovering that one's way of life is simply a dead end would, as Brooks suggests, lead anyone to feel that God had forsaken them, particularly when they had been promised more from life. But faith lies in this exact place, in the pressure to continue believing in life in the face of death. Life's meaning, therefore, is not a secularized hope in the persistence of our culture's way of life into the future, carried on by our children. Instead, it is the release of children from the burden of significance for us. Christian faith recognizes in Abraham the trust that God will find ways of being faithful to his promises apart from obligation or duty—astonishingly, ours and that of our children.

chapter seven

Until He Comes

Christians confess and look forward to the return of Christ. They set their minds toward God's good and gracious judgment on all things, a judgment that will be exercised in order for things to be put right, for the truth to be heard about the reality of everything that has championed or has been championed by falsehood, and for the weeping and groaning of loss to cease and instead be filled with mercy, goodness, and abundantly good things. The Christian anticipation of these things corresponds to their manner of living, though not primarily by way of receiving a reward while others receive their due punishment. The last judgment in which Christ judges as king is not a Christian version of karma in which "you get what you deserve" is shown to be the law of the cosmos after all.

This Christian hope has its antecedents and original theological orientation in the apocalyptic expectations of Judaism. Particularly expressed by her prophets, Israel looked forward to "the Day of the Lord," an unspecified time in future history when God will enact universal judgment against all of the nations in climactic fulfillment of the covenants made with Israel's forefathers. Blessing and the fulfillment of promises also has a reverse side for the opponents of God's ways, as Amos makes plain. "Woe to you who desire the day of the LORD! Why would you have the day of the LORD? It is darkness, and not light" (Amos 5:18). This day, for the Old Testament, was not envisioned as an atemporal moment beyond death and outside of the ordinary march of human history. The vectors of the nations will be directed toward Zion, the city that will gather the world according to the law and instruction of the Lord that has gone forth from it (Isa 2:2–4). The nations will summarily be judged according to that word while the forces (such as war) that separate the nations from each other will be replaced by activities (such as agriculture) that grow, heal, and bring together without fear (Mic 4:1–5). God's justice, on that day, creates peace marked by righteousness.

For the afflicted and weak (as Israel is often portrayed at the hands of her enemies), God promises a judgment that brings down the strong. This is the fate of Babylon in Isaiah 13: "They come from a distant land, from the end of the heavens, the LORD and the weapons of his indignation, to destroy the whole earth. Wail, for the day of the LORD is near; as destruction from the Almighty it will come!" (13:5–6). For these, the Day of the Lord promises to be destructive and agonizing, full of cruelty and anger (vv. 6–9), while Israel will be restored according to God's compassion (Isaiah 14). The overriding image is of God judging, not primarily for the sake of punishment, but for the sake of restoration and peace, or raising up the weak who cannot do it themselves and granting them the life of esteem and favor that God, out of divine kindness, means for them to have. "[W]ith righteousness he shall judge the poor, and decide with equity for the meek of the earth" (Isa 11:4). Needless to say, the Old Testament frequently shows Israel to be the object of God's wrath for the sake of justice for those entrusted to her care. Because of the special covenant that God made with Israel rather than with the other nations, Amos prophesies that that covenant's requirements will be roused and enforced (Amos 3:2; cf. Zeph 1:4–9).

Israel's expectation of God's deliverance from her enemies were messianic in that they looked for one who would act as the specific agent of this restoration. The Messiah is a king who brings justice and righteousness by singling out and vindicating the weak and vulnerable whom the strong have abused and exploited (e.g., Isaiah 11). Ezekiel's charge that Israel's leadership had been feeding themselves on the sheep entrusted to their care met with decisive censure. God the Lord will step in and be the shepherd that Israel was failing to provide. "I myself will be the shepherd of my sheep, and I will make them lie down, says the Lord God. I will seek the lost, and I will bring back the strayed, and I will bind up the injured, and I will strengthen the weak, but the fat and the strong I will destroy. I will feed them with justice. . . . I shall judge between sheep and sheep, between rams and goats" (Ezek 34:15–17). To judge is to make all of the distinctions that have not been made. It is to make known the overlooked misdeeds and atrocities as well as the unsung mercies and benevolent yet weak acts. For God sees those things that are opaque to incessant human striving and aggression. Those who take comfort that God is watching are the only ones whom we would expect will welcome the arrival of the king and with alacrity rush to his side when he comes. Christianity's eschatological expectation in this regard is the more specific hoping after things foretold through Israel's prophets.

If Ezekiel is to be believed, this act of judgment is at one with salvation itself. "I will save my flock, and they shall no longer be ravaged; and I will judge between sheep and sheep. I will set up over them one shepherd, my servant David, and he shall feed them: he shall feed them and be their shepherd" (Ezek 34:22–23). To be saved *is* to receive the consolation of justice against the reprobating forces of the world. Against this background, the Christian hope for judgment can be seen as primarily an expectation that the present inequities will cease once God reckons the goods and evils of the world according to the surpassing virtues of his gracious reign. "It is in the final judgment that dictators who may have been revered for their skill in statecraft are revealed as the tyrants that they were, and that the martyrs who died unknown and unburied are shown to be the true heroes of history."[1]

In Revelation, the slain martyrs cry out to God, "O Sovereign Lord, holy and true, how long before thou wilt judge and avenge our blood on those who dwell upon the earth?" (Rev 6:10). Their desperate hoping for the Day of the Lord is in marked contrast with those who dread its coming: "the kings of the earth and the great men and the generals and the rich and the strong" (v. 15). The return of Christ is thus a long-awaited consolation for those whose hoping has meant enduring the realities of falsehood, injustice, and loss. It is originally more about the hope of victims than the threat of punishment. It was first the expectation that God will not finally forget the innocent before it understood divine justice as the eschatological warning that sets itself against all of humanity.[2] The fact that its meaning and emphasis have changed throughout the centuries, at least in theology, may simply reveal the fact that this theology has

---

1. Bauerschmidt, *Holy Teaching*, 252 n. 11.
2. Cf. Moltmann, *Way of Jesus Christ*, 334–38.

not tended to be produced by history's victims. The various theologies of hope that the last half-century witnessed are aspects of this trend's long overdue redress. On this point alone, there is a very great irony, as I describe in the following paragraphs. The dialectic between un-expecting and hoping breaks down once God's coming justice is perceived to be punishment rather than resolution of wrongs suffered and reconciliation with those things that the wrongs have put out of reach for the time being.

Why must this setting right await the coming of Christ? If this hope is messianic, then all of Israel's expectations are also to be Christian ones. The Messiah does not merely restore the glory of David's rule. Rather, he takes everything that was good and just about a regime with its own admittedly mixed record and makes it the reality for all peoples and all times. The Lord brings a day that is also the end of all things with a final judgment that ends all judging.[3] It is not only a day for specific acts of judgment; its judgments end all judging.

What is new and distinctive about how the New Testament continues Israel's prophetic hope in other respects is that the judge is himself now identified.[4] "The Father judges no one, but has given all judgment to the Son" (John 5:22). Christians began to understand Isaiah's prophecy about the word of God going forth from Jerusalem in a christological manner. Jesus Christ did not simply bring the word of God as the prophets had done, but he fulfilled their words by himself going forth from Jerusalem in the body of the church. The saints are said one day to judge the world (1 Cor 6:2; yet also this is actually God's own act of judgment, 1 Cor 5:13). Yet God has also first judged Jesus himself through vindicating, by the resurrection, the kind of life that his was. The one who loved his enemies unto his own destruction receives God's judgment in his favor so that the love of enemies is itself also vindicated. Ought this to qualify how Christianity thinks about the universal, final judgment? Can the lover of enemies be the same one who oversees their final destruction? Only if the Father raised up the Son in a merely provisional act of judgment, the fullness of which will one day contradict it. But then is there not a problem of two Christs? Jesus would not so much already disclose to humanity the life of the Father; humanity must wait to see whether God is, after all, a lover of enemies. The promise that Christ will fulfill this role assures us

---

3. See Jenson, *Ezekiel*, 75.
4. See Jenson, *Systematic Theology*, 2:325.

of the answer.⁵ Paul declares as much to the Athenians: "[God] has fixed a day on which he will judge the world in righteousness by a man whom he has appointed, and of this he has given assurance to all men by raising him from the dead" (Acts 17:31).

Yet there is more going on in this revelation than simply the naming of the one tasked with the job to judge. If Jesus Christ will be the judge who restores all that has been broken in human community through the ruthless exercise of power and the perversion of justice, this is not to say that he is merely given responsibility for upholding the standards of equity, justice, and goodness, which throughout human history have repeatedly been overturned. It is rather that the one whose existence to Israel as that word from God which as the Law was intended to create a just nation is now *in his very person* the arbiter itself. Jesus will not judge according to anything other than himself. "Christ is himself the truth by which he judges."⁶ The New Testament teaches this from both sides: that Christ judges by his word (John 12:48) and that Christ himself is the one by which God judges (Rom 2:16). Christ does not reveal a standard of judgment other than himself; God's word of judgment is nothing other than Christ. And so we must bear in mind the life and work of Christ—the character of the judge—in order to understand the nature of the coming judgment. Indeed, there is no standard of judgment that is what it would have been without the cross and resurrection.⁷

Christ will be a King on his throne and surrounded by angels, as Matthew 25 describes. From his throne, the King will act as judge and advocate for the hungry, the thirsty, the naked, the stranger, and the prisoner. He will exercise and command this judgment on the basis of being one who was himself all of these things—strange and vulnerable to both those who confess him and those who do not. Jesus himself also did these things: he fed the hungry (Matt 14:13–21), cured the sick, comforted the sorrowful (15:21–28), and welcomed the stranger (8:5–13).

---

5. "Whatever the outcome of Christ's judgment of the living and the dead—whether all will be saved or only a few—this is *Jesus's* judgment, and Christians can wait for it only in the light of the gospel of Jesus Christ which they know and believe. But this Jesus does not come to judge. He comes to raise up. That is the messianic interpretation of the expectation of Christ's judgment" (Moltmann, *Way of Jesus Christ*, 338). Moltmann cites C. Blumhart, who wrote that "Jesus can judge, but not condemn."

6. Ibid., 326.

7. Ibid.

Therefore, longing for his return is most genuine among those whose profile of vulnerability Christ shares. In the time we inhabit, when suffering from some kind of injustice is the common lot of the world's majority, human suffering actually signals that God in Christ is in our midst. As Moltmann comments, the wretched "are the latent presence of the coming Savior and Judge in the world, the touchstone which determines salvation and damnation."[8] What, then, shall we say about those who are not suffering but who claim to want Christ's return? Do they know what they are asking for? Could it be that their lives have all along been more kingly than despised, more powerful than weak, and more commanding than serving? Will they therefore very readily recognize Christ as the King, jubilantly rising to meet him in his coming, perceiving with absolute clarity that Christ is on their side as they have assumed him to be all along? These are disturbing questions for those of us, like myself, who enjoy first-world comfort. It is possible that these same ones will be puzzled by the judgment that Jesus, as King, comes to make (v. 44), since having made a mistake in knowing him as strong, they continue that mistake in expecting a winning judgment for themselves.

By contrast, the ones who are praised, commended, and rewarded in this prophecy are exactly those who unexpected Jesus. It is those who are puzzled in exactly the opposite way who are commended. But the way these ones did not recognize Jesus in their care for the vulnerable ones differs quite a lot from the others who did not show compassion and care. Confronted with a kingly Jesus, they are puzzled that he was ever among the wretched of the earth. He only has to remind them that he is the same one as before. "When did we see you hungry and feed you?" They ask this because kings are well fed. The big surprise here is not really that a king was once vulnerable; it is that kingliness would be given to one from among vulnerable ranks. It is crucial to the identity of the risen Lord that Christianity confesses that Jesus is *still* among the wretched of the earth. He has not been glorified out of it. The incarnation is not over—Jesus Christ is still Jesus of Nazareth, a Jewish carpenter's son. One point of his glorification to the kingly throne (there is surely more than one) is that this elevation is the first of many, the rising of all of the weak and despised and oppressed (as Mary prayed, Luke 1:46–55).

The glorification of one of the wretched of the earth (a term used by Frantz Fanon that conveys the gist of the Hebrew *anawim*) is therefore

---

8. Moltmann, *Church in the Power of the Spirit*, 127.

the beginning of glorifying all of them. Jesus was not only raised from death; he was raised against the typical ascendency of the strong, who excel at beating others down. At the hand and good will of the Father, he is risen up in opposition to every unjust verdict, every unsavory and disreputable preference for power and wealth and privilege. The Son of God's glorification is itself the ultimate and final chastisement of glorification as the world knows it. The hardest thing, then, is to believe that the one who now exercises power and judgment is the same one who was most notably subject to the power and judgment of others. This is what makes the prophecy about the vulnerable ones confusing for both parties—those who expected Christ to be king all along and those who are shocked that a king would have anything at all to do with vulnerable life. (Just consider how unexpected it is for a king to be seen separating animals like a shepherd.) In Jon Sobrino's words, "The surprise felt by human beings on hearing that the Son of Man was incarnated in the poor is a surprise we must feel to comprehend the divinity of God on the cross."[9] There are both salutary and unsalutary reasons to be surprised. The difference is between being surprised that this kingly one is still the unconditional friend of publicans and sinners and that this kingly one ever would have been.

Even so, it is crucial that there is surprise in both cases. In the unsalutary version, the surprise comes (paradoxically) from the dogged attempt to shut down surprise as a possibility. It arises from a certainty in all those things in which power consists: that the strong will always prevail over the weak, that kings can do as they please, that those who possess power continually do favors for their powerful friends, and that they live lives of comfortable distance from material hardship and suffering. They are surprised that a king would have ever walked in the slums, let alone been subject to its ravages and wretchedness.

This is one sense in which some have notoriously worked against letting Christ's return be a surprise—indeed, as he promised it would be: as a thief in the night (Luke 12:39). This is more of a temptation for those whose waiting is desperate than for those whose waiting is optional or a luxury. Those who are constantly yearning for God's good and just verdict—for the divine act of setting things right against the injustice of the strong—are the ones most likely to feel the pull that threatens to hasten through knowledge the arrival of the King. The strong, on the other hand,

---

9. Sobrino, *True Church and the Poor*, 222.

either do not need the king to arrive, or *if they think they do*, they have the wrong idea about what kind of king comes to them. Against both tendencies, the gospel counsels believers to be busy about the things of the kingdom. It is first and foremost counsel to the weak. And why be busy in this way? Why occupy the otherwise emptiness of waiting with works of mercy? It is because your attentiveness to such things, rather than your distraction from them, will actually be your best education in recognizing that the Jesus whom you will worship has been the one you have all along been serving. It is the schooling of your life best suited to the coming of the King since a king is known by his loyal subjects, though his coming may still come unexpectedly. There is no escaping the surprise of the King. There is only the matter of whether you will be prepared to be pleasantly surprised in finding that what you have been doing all along has actually been in God's service.

Yet should we not also wonder whether the surprise of the compassionate ones goes deeper than this? Origen taught that it was out of humility that the compassionate ones kept from announcing their deeds as praiseworthy, not that they had forgotten what they had done. Yet what if they not only did not forget, but in fact *never knew in the first place*? Perhaps they did not know the teaching of this prophecy. The mere fact of Jesus telling it this way suggests that they are *not* privy to this prophecy about what the end will be like. Perhaps they were not waiting for Jesus' return in any respect whatsoever. Could they actually signal for us the dangers of expectation? Did their *not* waiting enable and fortify their acts of mercy? Maybe they are simply and straightforwardly what we call people of good will, people who simply show tenderness and kindness to strangers and the weak. They did not recognize the King in the stranger because they only saw the stranger and this was enough.

What are we to make of this as ones who know this teaching? On its own, it appears to be a teaching that makes the King in some sense irrelevant. But there is no escaping that these are the King's words to those of us who are listening—they cannot really make him irrelevant for us. As I suggested in chapter 2, the *knowledge* this teaching from Matthew 25 imparts cannot really have to do with generating *sympathy* for the weak any more than the teaching aims to convert a love for Jesus Christ into a love for strangers. There can be no conversion like this. Love does not increase with greater knowledge. If we claim to love Christ but do not love strangers and enemies, we quite simply do not love Christ. This teaching confirms just how impossible this is. It is not a matter of being untrue to our love of Christ; it really is not a love for him whatsoever. Moreover, and more astounding still, overcoming this lack of love cannot be accomplished by disciplining one's sights to see Christ in these others. What good would that do anyhow? If it is not a love for others, after all, there is no love of Christ that can lead to it. So our situation is actually precisely the reverse (there may be no other possibility): if we do not see these others with love, we cannot see Christ.

Does this mean that some will see Christ despite themselves and even despite their avowed apathy (and even antipathy) toward the Christian faith? Will some see him more and better than many who continually speak and sing of Christ as their lord week after week? The former will still be surprised by this judgment in their favor. Yet their not seeing Christ in the ones on whom they had compassion made no difference to their acts of mercy and compassion. They were merciful and compassionate anyway.

> Not every one who says to me, "Lord, Lord," shall enter the kingdom of heaven, but he who does the will of my Father who is in heaven. On that day many will say to me, "Lord, Lord, did we not prophesy in your name, and cast out demons in your name, and do many mighty works in your name?" And then will I declare to them, "I never knew you; depart from me, you evildoers." (Matt 7:21–23)

What a surprise! Shall we say that seeing Christ as "Lord" can therefore, for some, be part of the problem? Might "Lord" actually be an impediment when it comes to understanding the content and meaning of the lordship of Jesus Christ? Christians confess Christ as lord and king, but apart from careful attention to the kind of lord and king he actually is, they will be led badly astray. Christ comes to redefine these words against their typical meaning, to rescue authority and sovereignty from the powerful of the world. He comes first, walking into the hills of Galilee, into the universe of the sons and daughters of Israel, and into the world ahead of and through the church. He does not come first *as* anything at all, since any such thing will ultimately then precede him in our minds and hearts, disabling his welcome and enabling his rejection. This is the case with *lord* and *king* as much as it is with *Christ* and *Messiah*. The true Messiah of God first refuses and refutes the label of Messiah in order, only after this is thoroughly and completely accomplished, to reinhabit the label with his astonishing reality as other than what we expected him to be. Our hopes are not first met in Jesus of Nazareth as God's Christ to us; our hopes are first dashed, devastated, and shattered. Our expectations go radically unmet. And the more we "knew" what we wanted and hoped for, the more disappointed we are likely to be.

The ability to see Christ may not actually come about by trying to see Christ. It may not even necessarily come about secondarily, through acts that serve two purposes (compassion and seeing). The seeing of Christ is actually nothing less than the recognition that strangers are neighbors and that the weak, vulnerable, and unimportant will be objects of my kindness and love. Or, better: seeing Christ is simply my love of them. Finally, there are plenty of people who are not Christians—some who may even reject Christianity—who do this. "When did we see you hungry and feed you?" the labor unionist will ask. The King will possibly answer, "When you stood arm in arm with the poor workers who only wanted a day's pay for a day's work, you stood arm in arm with me." Some people may be surprised by this, but they should not ultimately be shocked: there are many who will not be.

When the New Testament contemplates the coming of Christ in glory, it is usually with the intention of promoting the patient endurance of the faithful, exhorting them not to lose heart in the face of trials and persecutions (e.g., Rev 1:9). Moreover, the context for these statements is often eucharistic. As the church is broken down by the world, its members inhabit the promise of glory and vindication of the righteous that has first been fulfilled in the resurrection of Christ (1 Cor 15:20). The Eucharist revives and preserves the struggling church by making present to the community of faith the life of the one who lives now the future of all the saints.

An early Christian exhortation, attributed to Hippolytus, preserves this connection.

> Come, ye prophets, who were cast out for my name's sake. Come, ye patriarchs, who before my advent were obedient to me, and longed for my kingdom. Come, ye apostles, who were my fellows

in my sufferings in my incarnation, and suffered with me in the Gospel. Come, ye martyrs, who confessed me before despots, and endured many torments and pains. Come, ye hierarchs, who did me sacred service blamelessly day and night, and made the oblation of my honourable body and blood daily.[10]

The ones who consistently and repeatedly make Christ's sacrifice a reality in their own lives are welcomed to Christ's side in his kingdom. Hippolytus shows that there are many ways of doing this—waiting with expectation and longing, suffering in the body as a martyr, and celebrating and participating in the Eucharist. How should we understand the close relation being made between these things? For the first time in these pages, we must allow some space for focusing on something that the church truly anticipates, something that has in no sense already happened, in no way is now present, dialectically or otherwise. When the church prays, "Come, Lord Jesus," it is genuinely praying for something that has not yet occurred. Yet, as I have repeatedly stressed, the church's ability to recognize Christ's coming when it happens will depend on how faithfully it has remembered, rehearsed, and inhabited Christ's life, death, and resurrection as past events. This Jesus whom Christians await already has a past. This is why the character of the coming judgment is already disclosed in the life, death, and resurrection of the judge.

I have intentionally prefaced a reflection on the eucharistic Christ and the church's eucharistic activities with this account of anticipation as the busyness of Christian living as compassionate care for the vulnerable. Historically, Christianity has not always and everywhere been on its guard to preserve this aspect of its communion celebration. Even though it is a meal characterized by the transformation of our meager gifts to God into God's abundant giving back to us, the Eucharist has nevertheless in Christian hands often overemphasized other aspects such as metaphysical ones. The fact of Christ's real presence in the Eucharist is indeed a mysterious miracle. But the real grace in it surely has just as much to do with that fact that through it God feeds the hungry with good things and redistributes material goods to everyone regardless of social rank as it has to do with the transformation of substances. Colombian theologian Rafael Avila notes the frequent disjunction between the church's celebration of the Eucharist as material sharing of resources and its professed belief

---

10. In *Ante-Nicene Fathers*, 5:252.

in its spiritual significance: "It is a sacrilege, according to St. Paul, when a Christian community, after having received the same bread and the same wine, continues to maintain social, economic, and cultural differences under the pretext that a mystical unity has been established."[11] That the church has allowed itself to be more captivated by the one miracle compared to the other tells us more about the church than it does about God. It reveals a church dangerously at risk of abandoning one of the central activities in the life of God. After all, God's life was in Christ being given for the wretched of the earth; in the Eucharist it still is.

When Christians break bread and drink wine together, they are re-enacting the manner in which their very existence as the church was created. They are also sustained by it to be the kind of people, not only who can remember rightly, but also who prevent themselves from straying from the foundation and source of their very constitution. So to remember rightly *is* to submit to and hope for the transformation as a people that is appropriate to the transformation of the Eucharist and the glorification of the Son of God whose death is vividly being celebrated. Doing these things makes possible nothing other than the ability even to call Christ's death a glorious event.

The church, therefore, expects to encounter more than Christ in the Eucharist. It also expects to encounter itself. As the body of Christ, the church also receives Christ's body. But it is only the former because it engages in the latter. The church is not the body of Christ *before* it is made into this through its corporate reception of the gift of God's self eucharistically. Its corporate identity is, in fact, what it receives. These two meanings of "the body of Christ" collapse in a way that Paul clearly knew about and intended in 1 Corinthians, a point on which I will elaborate below.

Now, if the church encounters itself in its encounter with the eucharistic Christ, then its own corporate self is as other to itself as Christ is. The heterogeneous character of the church (though *not* its lack of unity) is actually part of what it means to be the body of one whose risen living is bound to be full of surprises. This is clear from Paul's description of the church as Christ's many-membered body. The multiplicity of the parts of the body, with the corresponding gifts required to be themselves, is one

---

11. Avila, *Worship and Politics*, 100. The story of how the meaning of the body of Christ changed throughout history from church to host is told by de Lubac in *Corpus Mysticum*. For an extraordinary account of the significance of de Lubac's work in this regard, see Hollon, *Everything Is Sacred*, ch. 3.

with the reality of the risen Christ's freedom to be himself to and for the church. (The reason that lack of unity fails to witness to the heterogeneous character of the church is obvious: it witnesses instead to a Christian impatience with the corporate living that being one body demands.)

One of the great mysteries surrounding the body of Christ is the clever theological use that Paul, in particular, makes of it. He follows a sacramental logic that folds the meaning of a sacrament into the action the sacrament performs. What a sacrament does is, in fact, to convey the thing that it signifies. But the theological tradition has typically taken measures to make clear that they accomplish this without completely reducing the sign (*signum*) to the thing (*res*). Paul writes about the body of Christ in the same way. The bread and cup are, for Christians, the ways that we share in the body and blood of Christ, and our sharing in them is the way that we—who are many—are made into one body, the church (1 Cor 10:16–17). This alone is a profound turn of theological concepts. As Augustine taught, whereas everything else we eat becomes a part of us—of our bodies—the Eucharist is the only thing that, in eating it, we become part of it.[12] The bread, therefore, while not completely identified with the church (since we do not eat the church), nevertheless is the means of our sharing in the unity of Christ's members. And the ways that we share in it at least partially figure what it brings about. This is why our eating of it is done together (there is no private Eucharist) and is a meal of fellowship.[13] The sharing of bread works together with the sacramental action of sharing *in* the bread.

Again, what this means for the church is that Paul intends for us not to be able to conceive of one without the other—neither the church without the Eucharist, nor the Eucharist without the church. Paul does not simply mean two things when he identifies both the church and the bread as the body of Christ. He means to make them inseparable although not altogether identified. The well-known story of the dispute between Radbertus and Ratramnus, two ninth-century theologians, involves the emperor

12. Augustine, *Confessions*, VII.10.

13. There is a minority exception to this made in the tradition. In early centuries, it was permitted in cases of persecution for the sacrament to be kept and consumed privately. After the Council of Toledo (480 AD) denounced the practice of not consuming the Eucharist immediately after its consecration, the practice disappeared. See "Reservation of the Blessed Sacrament." In persecution, the body of the church is fractured by external forces and so the unity the sacrament conveys and enacts is a future one for which the Eucharist itself yearns.

Charles the Bald asking, "Is the body and blood of Christ there only as symbolised or in fact?" Radbertus answered, "Both," and this summarily has been the church's main answer.[14] Even though Huldrych Zwingli's view that the Eucharist is merely a remembrance ceremony has caught on more widely than in just the churches that claim him as a theological ancestor, it is perhaps just as important to resist the other extreme, whereby the symbolic value of the Eucharist is so depleted that what it is "in fact" is unduly elevated (or, put differently, there is all *res* and no *signa*). It is obvious that Christians do not eat and drink the church; but more subtly, the church makes declarations by its sacramental acts that do the pointing-to work that signs do as well as show us and others the significance of what is happening through them. Both of these things are crucially *in addition to* being the graces that the sacraments bring and impart.

One paradigmatic gospel way of approaching the resurrection ahead of its actual occurrence is, not coincidentally, a meal. The miracle of the loaves and fishes has elements that prefigure the kind of remembering that the Last Supper will institute formally. As a feeding story, it is related to the stories of Jesus healing the blind and lame, complete with the miraculous meal that disregards the limits of what the disciples' money could buy, beginning instead only with what they had ("How many loaves have you? Go and see" [Mark 6:38]). Yet it is also different from the healing stories in that the crowds were not starving to death nor simply so poor that Jesus' provision of a meal was their only hope. The disciples, after all, had suggested the most reasonable solution: it was getting to be dinnertime and Jesus ought to send the crowds away so that they can go into the surrounding villages and buy themselves something to eat (Mark 6:36). Jesus' reply—"You give them something to eat" (Mark 6:37)—recasts the problem, not primarily as one of hunger and eating, but as one of unity, sharing, and gift-giving. Following the disciples' suggestion would have meant the fragmentation of the church, everyone going away on their own to fend for themselves, no longer at the feet of Jesus. In contrast, Jesus' solution preserves the church community as those crowds who look to Jesus for more than just teaching, but also for sustaining them into the night.

14. Cited in Jenson, "Church and the Sacraments," 213.

It is in this way that this feeding story from the Gospels shows itself also to be a story about the Eucharist and a way of anticipating the Last Supper from within the gospel narrative. When God feeds his people with the body of Christ, the church is constituted as the body of Christ; the crowds are transformed into the church (or at least prefigure and symbolize it); those who would formerly feed themselves submit to God's unpredictable yet abundant gifts. When Christians look to Jesus only for teaching, hungering for advice, they merely reproduce the posture of the crowds and the expectations of Jesus' disciples. But when they recognize that their being together, and together with Jesus, is a matter of trust and giving and receiving—when they begin to hunger for other things—they are acting like a church. This is a reminder that, while one temptation is always to imagine that one can live by bread alone, as Jesus himself was tempted to think (Luke 4:4), the near-opposite is also the case: the temptation to believe that bread comes of our own work, that it is less spiritual because it is for the body and not the soul, that it is the object of an efficiency that sends people away from Jesus into separate villages and homes. The true place for bread is, as Christians have always confessed, with the others who are kept close to Jesus through God's giving of God's own self. We come to understand the real meaning of bread through sharing it with those others with whom Jesus has likewise shared it, which is only to say both that the Eucharist is the paradigmatic meal and that it is, as such, a meal of unity.[15]

It is here that we can begin to appreciate what all of this has to do with the resurrection. Like any good story, the gospel (in the Gospels, especially) gives readers and hearers narrative clues that anticipate the climax of the story. When Jesus sustains the crowds as a church by feeding them in the wilderness rather than sending them away into the villages, we are confronted with a profound eucharistic reality that only makes sense in light of the resurrection, the latter itself an event that comes later in the story. It also reveals that there is more going on than an act in which the church is created and sustained by God's food of Christ; the church's unity actually depends on the breaking and sharing of that food. The crowds do not break apart at mealtime; instead the

---

15. The idea of the Eucharist as the paradigmatic meal shows how it does not merely *reflect* unity but *effects* it. It also implies that the Eucharist does no less than what meals are supposed to do. Our ideas of eating together flow from it rather than the reverse. When the Eucharist fails to be a meal of unity, all other eating is distorted.

church is gathered for and by the breaking of the meal, its proliferation and distribution.

I am once again simply alluding to the miracle that makes the Eucharist a sacrament. It is the miracle that is God's action within it. As a story of excess, this Gospel feeding story does not merely highlight the abundance of all "natural" things, but it crucially locates God's life within the life of creation as one of continuous giving and creating.[16] Any natural thing can take part in God's sacramental uses since all natural things are what Christians describe as creatures, as dependent on God for their existence and therefore at his complete and utter disposal.

The resurrection, therefore, may be spoken of as Christ's *multiplication*. It is the site of his abundant presence—more accurately, *re*-presence—against life's scarcity, death. The resurrected Christ is promised to fill the earth, evoking all the resonances of the biblical tradition. It calls to mind God's directive that Adam and Eve not delay in providing the earth its fullness of their offspring. It also evokes God's promise to Abraham that his descendants would be as numerous as the stars in the sky. As Israel believes God's promises to be true and trusts therefore that he will faithfully accompany that nation in such an unlikely project against the pressures, tragedies, and unlikely destinies of living among the other nations, it presses most determinatively against the way of life that knows only the scarcity of limited resources and one-to-one correspondences. If Israel's trust explodes the constraining logic, it becomes a witness to the God of promised abundance and multiplication.

Here in Christ, Israel's hopes in God's promises are most acutely focused. God "gifts" Christ to the world through the multiplication of loaves and fishes. The people gather, eat, and are satisfied. They not only share a meal of bread in an ordinary sense, however, since as a eucharistic story, the "host" is both the giver and the gift, the means of the multiplication and its substance. This is the root miracle of the loaves and the fishes, and it is precisely a eucharistic one: God is made present to his people as his own very life, meeting his own promises neither through command nor obedience but in over-giving (giving again and making possible) the material conditions that make the actions into completed promises. Israel's most fundamental covenants are fulfilled in Christ's multiplication for the nations.

---

16. If this is what one intends by "natural," then I have no objection. But it is often not.

Now, if this is a vision of how the church shares its eucharistic meal together, then it is not actually bounded only by the resurrection. It plays a double role also as a story of how the church is to live expectantly for Christ's return in glory. A communion prayer in the *Didache* reads: "As this bread was dispersed over the mountains, and has been gathered into one, so may your church be gathered from the ends of the earth in your kingdom." Christians participate in this scattering and gathering according to the hope that what God has sown will in due course come together again.

What has been scattered is gathered back in a harvest. According to Gerhard Lohfink, this is the persistent theme of the whole Bible and the best way to understand what the salvation of Israel and the rest of humanity entails. William Cavanaugh summarizes that, according to Lohfink, "gathering the many into one is the form that salvation takes in the world. Scattering is not only the consequence of sin, as in the Babel story, but scattering defines sin—sin is the breakup of the original unity of creation."[17] Lohfink points out that Israel understood the exile in Babylon to be its own scattering and yearned to be regathered from among the nations, using the language of salvation in their prayer (Ps 106:47). Jesus continues the theme by taking on himself the mantle of gatherer: "he who does not gather with me scatters" (Matt 12:30). In Jesus' teaching the one who scatters is a wolf; the one who gathers is a shepherd (John 10:12).[18] Finally, the New Testament goes even further, portraying Christ as the one in whom the gathering takes place—in and as his very body (1 Cor 12:13). In the *Didache* (4:3), the church is spoken of as the scattered bread that has now been regathered from the ends of the earth and made one. The difficult lesson and reality for Israel was to discover God beyond its borders. The New Testament teaches what is a development of Old Testament trajectories so that, with Jesus Christ, nations are not streaming to a place—Jerusalem and the Temple—but to a person, becoming part of the church of Jews and Gentiles now grafted into Israel, together now a "chosen race, a royal priesthood, a holy nation, God's own people" (1 Pet 2:9).

---

17. Cavanaugh, *Migrations of the Holy*, 146. Cavanaugh is summarizing Lohfink, *Does God Need the Church?*

18. There are many more examples of this motif that we could cite. For example, in a passage in which John discusses how we ought to understand Jesus' death in the face of the high priest's prophecies, John summarizes that Jesus' death takes the place of his whole nation: "and not for the nation only, but to gather into one the children of God who are scattered abroad" (John 11:52).

Unexpected Jesus

The themes of exile and diaspora are important to the work of John Howard Yoder, who often emphasized that, beginning most intensely with Jeremiah, Israel's message to the nations was also the most difficult one for it to learn—that "dispersion is mission."[19] Reflecting on the meaning of Jeremiah's call for the exiles in Babylon to "seek the welfare of the city where I have sent you into exile" (Jer 29:7), Yoder comments, "[T]here was never reason for debate about whether the shalom was knowable to the Babylonians, or about whether it was relevant. The need was for the Jewish exiles themselves to believe that that was their mission."[20] Scattering is mission and the way God's people are made to reckon with a God who enlists his scattered own *by himself also being among the scattered* in order to reach a scattered world.

The goal is always return, gathering, and harvest. Only now what has been divided and scattered is transformed into a new kind of life—the seed changing into fruit and grain, the workers doing the harvest work, a very common theme in the Gospels. The ordinary things of God's creation will neither be obliterated nor erased when all things are made new. They will be reshaped, retold, and re-storied according to God's triumphant Lamb. They will not be lost.

So it is possible to see in this miracle of feeding the crowds in Galilee a foretaste or prefiguring of the church's mission that in fact fulfills and continues to fulfill God's promise to the other nations through Israel by way of Christ's apostles. The way this actually happens is in the scattering of the apostles in their mission. When Jesus quotes "I will strike the shepherd, and the sheep of the flock will be scattered" (Matt 26:31), it becomes plain that scattering initially indicates, not the mission of the apostles, but the manner in which, in Jesus' words in the same verse, "you will all fall away because of me." Yet like the dispersal of Israel into exile in Babylon, it is turned around for missionary purposes in the discovery that God will be found in new and farther-flung places. Indeed, the salutary scattering of the apostles only occurs through the momentum of resurrection, as Jesus predicts next: "But after I am raised up, I will go before you to Galilee" (v. 32). Their going out is initially a shameful disunity, but in the movements set in motion by the action of God raising Jesus from the dead, it is a sending, a commissioning. Apostles burst from the upper room where, ironically, they had in fact "gathered," though for no evangelistic purpose.

19. Yoder, *For the Nations*, 52.
20. Ibid., 34.

The reader potentially wonders why they have not gone to Galilee. Would this not have begun their mission? (Jesus' promise to go ahead of them away from Jerusalem is part of Mark's and Matthew's story [Mark 16:7 and Matt 28:7].) With the start of Acts (1:8), the apostles are summarily sent to all the nations, beginning with Jerusalem, paralleling Christ bursting from the tomb. In this, the center of gravity shifts from Jerusalem as the place the resurrection is *from* to the farthest reaches of the earth—the very places the resurrection yearns to reach. Christianity understands Israel's gathering to itself true worshippers to be the true worship of God by every nation, radically relativizing the places this is meant to happen.

Once again, it is part of Yoder's argument that this is part of Israel's self-understanding, even if it sometimes appears to arise within its Scripture as a lesson Israel is struggling more fully to appropriate. It is a lesson that the prophet Jonah could not learn even while the book of Jonah inserts it as a sharp reminder within Israel's prophetic tradition. When Jonah attempts to flee the "presence of the Lord" and finds that he cannot, he also finds out what it is like for the nations to repent where they are (as with the mariners on the boat in chapter 1 and with the people and animals of Nineveh in chapter 3). Jonah's flight was a gathering *because* it was a scattering. Reflecting on Jonah, Yoder writes, "When Jonah was told to go to Nineveh, his reason for going the other way was not the fear that his particular Hebraic worldview would seem sectarian or esoteric to the Ninevites, but rather the fear that they might hear and be saved, which is what we are told did happen."[21] So the New Testament intensifies the theme so that the gathering of the nations *is*, in a sense, already resident within the scattering. The gospel providentially translates "come" as "go" and embodies this impulse through its presence among the nations as bearers of the good news about Christ.

If so, then the church not only announces Christ but in fact "delivers" Christ, bringing not just words about him, but actually bringing him. This is what is involved in the Pauline theology in which Christ is more than the gatherer; he is the site of the gathering—the church is the body of Christ. This is therefore the crucial dialectic that the church's eucharistic mysteries somehow manage to hold together. Christ is present in the church—we even say *as* the church—yet in a way that surpasses it. Christ is delivered by the church's ministry, and yet that ministry, if it is to be true, always

21. Ibid.

points beyond the church toward Christ as stranger to both church and world, believer and unbeliever alike. The dialectic is one in which Christ is both really present in the church and really present beyond it.

This is why I suggest that the gospel's scattering is the form of its gathering. In this mode, its movements are out rather than in, expansive rather than contractive, edging toward what is unknown rather than shoring up what is known. Again, this shifting of the balances does not signal a reduced confidence in the things Christianity knows. Instead, it refigures Christian knowledge as a faith in promises that will never entirely be put into the past and so must always be spoken of in at least the present tense (when it is not speaking in the future tense). In other words, Christian knowing is more like living, walking, and loving than having, keeping, and owning. Its assurances are movements, the confidence that something is happening, that a faculty is being exercised. Christ is "multiplied" and, just so, scattered by the work of God in making him a living presence to the church. This is the very odd kind of news the resurrection constitutes for Christianity, yet it is essential to its being true. The more it is known merely as an event, the less it is known in its truth as the object of confession.

chapter eight

Theology and Surprise

In the preceding chapters, I have tried to reveal aspects of the interplay between knowing and unknowing that comes with encountering the life of Jesus Christ in his resurrection. The more he is known to be the Christ, the one who authentically and decisively reveals God, the more he will be recognized in this identity when he is seen. But for precisely the same reason, the things that make him the unique and unsurpassable revelation of the Father are the case for one whose living requires *unknowing*, a felicity for real-time encounter with surprise. As Gregory of Nyssa taught regarding God's beauty, it "is always seen as something new and strange in comparison with what the mind has always understood. And as God continues to reveal himself, man continues to wonder."[1]

There are, no doubt, peculiarities to this interplay between knowing and unknowing since we have been considering Jesus' uniqueness in many respects. But its most significant aspects turn out not to be all that particular to him at all since they are characteristics of what is involved in knowing any living person. The life of Jesus will be found in strangers, as he promises, since our not knowing him is quite a lot like our not knowing other people whom we do not know.

While the chapters have, up to this point, focused either on the interplay between Jesus and the church or the Christian, I want in this final chapter to look at whether and how theology can be a discipline of

1. Gregory of Nyssa, *Homilies on the Song of Songs*, in *From Glory to Glory*, 246. I gratefully owe my awareness of this quotation to the work of Will Cohen.

un-expectation—what it would mean to be alert, to discipline its methods in order to stay awake, and to open itself to the surprises demanded by its object of study. There is an immediate problem with speaking about theology as a discipline. Every discipline strives to match its modes of investigation to its subject matter. To be sure, both confessionally and etymologically, theology's subject matter is God. Yet we can identify at least four substitutes for God when it comes to defining theology's task, particularly when we look at that wider umbrella of Christian disciplines. They are history, theology itself, the Bible, and culture.

First is the temptation to take history as theology's subject matter. This temptation is strongest among history's winners. These are the ones with the most trenchant will to believe that the way things are is the way things ought to be, that the slow and steady progress of time is God's smile on those who appear to benefit, and that we see in history an unfolding of a divine plan, especially to the extent that some are able to see God's obvious blessing on their station and how they got there. It is a genuine Christian impulse to try to discover God in history since God in Christ has taken the history of creatures to be his own; the discipline of history helps to show how theology is thus how God has christologically inhabited history through human talk about God. Even so, humans notoriously err when we attempt to discern the general trends with greater clarity than is really possible. We are not the best judges of our own significance; we need to depend on others to interpret the meaning of our lives in God's world. Take the way that Scripture and extra-scriptural history relate to each other.

The many ways that the exodus has been claimed by others who saw God's hand in their own liberations from slavery and all kinds of oppression is itself an affirmation that God's acts can be discerned to be God's by how they reproduce other canonical events in history that we are assured were also God's doing. But there is a particular ambiguity that accompanies such interpretations. The liberated people and those who work for that liberation risk a certain amount of moral clarity about their own actions at the hands of others in the church who may or may not come along later and narrate their struggle as one with Christ's own, as sharing in what his work emancipates. Until this happens, those who act do so in the grey and fog of an incomplete history of God's people in the world. Knowing how the story will end does not automatically throw back over all human action the definitive and authoritative way to understand how

Theology and Surprise

what we do here will be a part of what is brought along to there. The distinct challenge is to be able to face the cynical temptation that says I can only act with confidence so long as my knowing how things are surpasses my hoping, not only that they are meant to be different, but that in so acting I also hope that others will see—better than I—that I acted rightly.

Second is the temptation to treat theology as the subject of its own inquiry. Is theology the same thing as the study of theology? In this mode, theology primarily studies *ideas* and the *people* who produced them. It asks whether the ideas are compatible and consistent with each other (theology as *systematic*), whether they are true to the God who is revealed in the Bible and with who Christianity, throughout the centuries, has confessed God to be.

The temptation is very strong. After all, no theologian works (or ought to work) in isolation from others. And she ought to be suspicious of new discoveries—not because God is not still speaking (God is), but because if God is the faithful one whom Christianity confesses, then ideas that are, in a sense, *too new* bear the burden of showing that God did not simply abandon our forebears to their errors. This is obviously a delicate balance. It is entirely possible that our forebears erred; but at the same time, if the church is made up of saints who are both living and dead, then those who are living bear the burden of keeping the dead within the church. They must enlarge the tradition they inherit rather than abandon it. The temptation of what is *too new* is to do the latter.

Yet it is easy for theology to see itself too much like the other disciplines if its primary work is the study of theology rather than God. The value of knowing Barth's doctrine of election or Anselm's doctrine of the atonement must not outweigh the questions they were asking.

Even so, in at least one sense, theology *is* indeed the study of theology. When it genuinely locates itself within the tradition of thinking about God that has preceded it, theology commits itself to pressing back against and extending that tradition, thereby disclosing its gratitude to what came before. Like any tradition of inquiry, theology does not consider slavish repetition to be an act of faithfulness. Rather, this requires the attempt to ask the old questions in new ways, to uncover the treasures of the theological inheritance for today's church, and to push the old answers up against new questions to see whether they suffice. As Hans-Georg Gadamer observes, the questions that others asked in the past are available to our ability to reconstruct the conditions in which they were asked, but we should not think that this means we will come to understand them. "Asking [someone else's question] opens up possibilities of meaning and thus what is meaningful passes into one's own thinking on the subject. Questions that we do not ourselves ask, such as those that we regard as out of date or pointless, are understood in a curious fashion. . . . For what we understand, in such cases, is precisely that there is no question." Rather, we only truly understand a question when it is also currently a question for us, something to which we want to know the answer. "To understand a question means to ask it."[2]

To continue to recognize some questions as openings in which we find ourselves is to belong to and inhabit a tradition of inquiry. We manifestly do *not* count ourselves members of a tradition because we have learned to supply the canonical answers. Instead, the questions the tradition has judged worth asking are the same ones that haunt us. In all of this, the theologian shows herself to be a faithful steward of the ways she has learned to speak. She may well end up surpassing those who taught her to speak this way, but only by way of having first learned to speak "Christian."

A third temptation is to turn theology into a mere servant of the Bible. Ever since the nineteenth century, the study of the Bible has developed in relative independence from the other theological disciplines, honing research tools and methods that are strange to theologians.

In former times, the study of the Bible flowed from theology since the latter provided the critical tools for interpreting it. The ways that Christians understood what they were doing when they talked about Christ fulfilling God's covenant with Israel provided them with ways of looking for Christ in the Old Testament as the covenant's anticipation and inner logic. However, recent history has seen this reversed: the meaning of the Bible is sought and elaborated prior to its (optional) use by theology. The first task is to elaborate the "biblical basis" or "biblical foundation" of a topic before theologians are permitted to do their work.

This temptation is very strong. Yet if the theological disciplines primarily study *texts*, they become antiquarian disciplines. But it is a Christian confession that the Word made flesh in Christ has been set free. He is therefore more appropriately encountered in personal form rather than textual form.

---

2. Gadamer, *Truth and Method*, 338.

Theology and Surprise

This in no way dismisses the importance of the Bible. Rather it points to the kind of reading to which the Bible lends itself when considered to be the church's Scripture (which is to say, when it is read by people who believe it to be God's Word, which is not everybody). For example, the Bible is first to be read liturgically, as the fund and fount for the church's language in praise, entreaty, and lament. During Holy Week, when the congregation cries out, "Crucify him!" it is recognizing that these words do not merely have historical value in telling us what a crowd chanted in Jerusalem two millennia ago (Mark 15:13, 14). Nor do these words simply have textual value in being part of the biblical narrative about Jesus, disclosing what can be known about him from the gospel story. Rather, this liturgical practice, the recitation in which congregation plays acrimonious mob, situates those who engage in it *within the narrative* that the text tells. It confesses that we are the enemies of God, that we rejected God's Messiah, and that we continue to do so. It also unites the church with Israel, preventing Gentile Christians from supposing that "His blood be on us and on our children!" (Matt 27:15) belongs only to Jews. Christians also enact this in the eucharistic celebration where, again because it is used liturgically, the Bible functions in its first role.

Can all of the theological disciplines locate themselves in the church's liturgical practice, in the life of the community of faith? When they do, they most genuinely find themselves dealing with what the Bible *means*, even discovering that this may differ from—and be in addition to—what it *meant*. Christianity is not only commited to studying the past, but does so (as it does everything else) for the present faithfulness of Christian people.

Fourth is the temptation to make theology a branch of cultural or social theory. Perhaps theology ought to devote itself to the study of the culture and cultures that Christianity has produced throughout the millennia. In fact, it very often does just this. Doing so differs from the study of history in being more forthcoming about its constructive (or deconstructive) aims. Like the others, this also is a very strong temptation. Religion is obviously a powerful cultural force and, for many who see the recent history of the West as characterized by a decline in culture, the cultural legacy to recapture is Christianity. The Roman Catholic Church, for example, in its battle with European secularization, reasserts Christianity's contributions to that heritage. (A current, frequent topic for theological inquiry has to do with the very great irony that Christianity produced the notion of the secular and found ways of encouraging various permutations that eventually learned to outgrow Christianity.[3])

Then again, not every instance of theology as cultural studies longs for the past. Just as often—especially in recent years—cultural studies exposes the power dynamics that those who have had the power have managed to hide from dominant forms of critique. In this mode, Christianity is studied as a form of *ideology*.

A collapse of Christianity into ideology is seemingly vindicated by observing that, with the decline of the former, we might also triumphantly celebrate the end of the latter. However, if literary critic Terry Eagleton is to be believed, then this recent move to declare the "end of ideology" is itself very much still the work of ideology. But it is a subtler and more dangerous form than the earlier critiques sought to identify since this one works by denying its own existence; the more it succeeds, the more it recedes from the discussion about what is going on. As an example of this success, Eagleton notes how the prophets of the end of ideology function to enervate what he sees as morally and politically praiseworthy about Marxism and socialism. This move does not endeavor to make room for a new kind of life—no-ideology—but its near-inverse. It signals and even paves the way for the victory of capitalism, itself an ideology that can claim that this kind of life is bare, normal, unadorned, and plain.[4]

When it is primarily, or largely, about culture, has theology ceased to be about God? Theology offers a way of narrating and framing what is most significant about cultures. Still, if God is truly theology's object, then its goal is not to explain things so much as to make us more faithful to God by subjecting our speech about him to great care and discipline.

No theology speaks the final word. It is not given to those who speak and write of the science of God to make definitive pronouncements.[5] Christians worship and follow a living God who, in Christ, continues to assert his freedom to surprise. This is not a shortcoming particular to theology, although theologians may find coming to terms with it more

---

3. See the work of Radical Orthodoxy (particularly John Milbank and Catherine Pickstock), Charles Taylor, and so on. Oliver O'Donovan is involved in a similar project of recovery in Christian political thought. See his *Desire of the Nations*. Much of this investigation centers on some technical matters in the work of Augustine. See, for example, Markus, *Saeculum*, and Williams, "Politics of the Soul."

4. See Eagleton, *Ideology*.

5. Though then statements like this one cannot avoid the appearance of contradiction.

difficult than some others. Yet what then about those many attempts by the church to set out timeless (though clearly set out *in time*) dogmatic formulations as correctives against false teaching and as gifts and guarantors for future generations of Christians? In particular, once again, what shall we say about the creeds?

The church's adoption of the creeds, rightly understood, are ways it has found to be faithful theologically to the church's worship practice. In the case of the Trinitarian debates in the fourth century, Rowan Williams reflects on the way that, as inheritors of the victorious tradition, we can be misled into imagining a straightforward case in which "the church" opposed a single, coherent party of heretics. To the contrary, such debates exemplify the church becoming self-aware intellectually and no longer able to continue with a "theology of repetition."[6] In order to do so, the church found itself needing to go outside of its scriptural and liturgical language, borrowing terminology from Greek philosophy in order to say of God what it took to be the genuine theological convictions that it had always held. Then as now, this move struck many as a departure. "Athanasius' task is to show how the break in continuity generally felt to be involved in the creedal *homoousios* is a necessary moment in the deeper understanding and securing of tradition; more yet, it is to persuade Christians that strict adherence to archaic and 'neutral' terms alone is in fact a potential betrayal of the historic faith."[7]

Creeds are not meant to specify the definitive language within which God will be spoken (an impossibility if God is still speaking, as in Christ) nor to lay out the absolute and unqualified idioms within which the acts of God will be recognized. Rather they are tools for clarifying, against other contemporary ideas, what the church more frequently confesses using other language. As Rowan Williams teaches, "The Church's theology begins in the language of worship, which rightly conserves metaphors and titles that are both ancient and ambiguous; but it does not stop there. The openness, the 'impropriety,' the *play* of liturgical imagery is anchored to a specific set of commitments as to the limits and defining conditions within which the believing life is lived, and the metaphorical or narrative beginnings of theological reflection necessarily generate new attempts to characterize those defining conditions."[8] Christians can only,

6. Williams, *Arius*, 235. Williams credits the specific phrase to Georges Florovsky.
7. Ibid.
8. Ibid., 235–36.

in some limited sense, claim their understanding of the language "Son of God" on account of how they use it liturgically to refer to Jesus Christ. But since every title, as Williams insists, is involved in free play within a larger set of imagery and use in practice, with repetition, Christians will only (ironically, perhaps) be left with these specific ways of speaking. Therefore, theology serves the mission of the church as the church spreads to new linguistic settings by providing it with new language in which to say what it has been saying all along. Innovation is the necessary corollary to the will to preserve; the conservative and progressive impulses are one in Christianity, as they really are in any tradition that takes its original idioms seriously. According to Williams, this means that theology is tasked to help Scripture and tradition both become stranger and more difficult, highlighting what is not obvious about them, in order to continue to use them truthfully in new settings and new ages.[9]

Furthermore, the creeds are tools for the future imagination. They identify with care the manner in which God has spoken in order to attune those who confess them to the continuing, ensuing, and impending speech that the church commits itself to developing. They locate the church (rather than, say, the academy) as the site of theological reflection. Councils and creeds, in so attuning Christian hearts, also impress on themselves and those who follow after them the conviction that God in Jesus Christ has not only spoken to the church but has crucially spoken the church into being. Christ's presence in and to the church is, as I have tried to show in previous chapters, perhaps the most complex way that Christians encounter the interplay between knowing and unknowing. The church does not simply and straightforwardly busy itself with other things while it waits for Christ who will come from the outside. Neither does the church possess the one whom God sent to it in the past. Rather, the church countenances Christ always in the present tense as one who is known first as one knows anybody else, and is known only secondarily as a deposit. Christ is not simply a stranger any more than he is merely an object of the church's devoted energies in its rounding up, gathering, and holding the things it calls its own. The situation is more complex than this because the church itself (in its subjectivity to the things it "has") *as given* may partially be the locus from which it receives gifts. The first gift the church receives is itself, and this only makes sense if being the church is

---

9. Ibid., 236.

something best spoken of as an identity it freely surrenders, knowing that it cannot come about by our anxious clutching.

The New Testament writers understood that the God of Israel's Scripture was the same as the God of Jesus Christ who, in continuing to speak—indeed as now speaking *himself*—discloses the true meaning of the Scriptures. Christ enables and entitles the church to look for Christ in all things, in unexpected places, beginning with Israel and her Scriptures. Crucial to this entitlement is the fact of the Old Testament as the church's Scripture. Jenson argues that it is a mistake to claim that Christians *adopted* the Old Testament, since this was never really up for debate.[10] The early heresy attributed to Marcion was noticeable because it was such a clear departure from the thinking of the New Testament church. Instead, the most pressing questions had to do with how to read the Scriptures the church knew they were in no position to abandon. Christ was the hermeneutical key (or "critical theory") for their reading.

When Matthew's Gospel cites the fulfillment of "out of Egypt have I called my son" (Hos 11:1. Matt 2:15), it displays Christianity's confidence in discovering the continuity between Israel and Christ. Originally, it referred to Israel as God's son, yet Matthew interprets its full meaning to lie in Christ. How is Israel "God's son"? And how is it revealed in Christ's sonship? As Jenson argues, "[T]he Son indeed precedes his human birth without being simply unincarnate: the Son appears as a narrative pattern in the history of Israel." Also, "What in eternity precedes the Son's birth to Mary is not an unincarnate *state* of the Son, but a pattern of movement within the event of the Incarnation, the movement to Incarnation, as itself a pattern of God's triune life."[11] In other words, Christ does not extend a metaphor to which Israel gives definitive meaning. But the reverse: Christ is the true meaning of Israel's sonship. The world's rejection of Christ, then, is Israel's own refusal to be the people who inhabit God's purposes for themselves. Christians have never assumed that the idea that God has a son is something with an obvious meaning. Israel's sonship is crucial to how God discloses this. It is something that is not disclosed to the world as a fact or idea (as though theology is what finally matters). The fact that God has a Son is disclosed in the very presence of the Son.

Likewise, just as the Word of God comes to the Hebrew prophets, God's speech to the world as Christ makes Christ himself more than a

10. Jenson, *Canon and Creed*, ch. 3.
11. Jenson, *Systematic Theology*, 1:141.

prophet. A prophet brings and witnesses to the word he hears; Christ is that word. If prophets exhort the people to turn from their wicked ways, it is in favor of pointing to and elaborating the way they were to walk instead. In Christ, the church confesses to locate God's word-presence among us as that way. It is a Christian skill (and one not easily mastered) to recognize that the thing God speaks when he speaks is the Son he sends. Christ is no mere teacher. Israel routinely rejected the prophets God sent to her and, in doing so, rejected God's word to Israel. But Israel did not only reject a word of instruction. She rejected her own story. The sons and daughters of Israel failed to be a people oriented around the life that God makes through covenants.

Jesus Christ "is the Word of God in that he is the narrative content of the proclamation that, because it poses eschatological possibility, is the Word of God. He is the Word of God because he is the narrative content of the word-event that is the Word of God."[12] If this is so, then Jesus does not only fulfill the law through obedience to instructions that the sons and daughters of Israel did not obey. Rather, his existence is irreducibly historical, and everything that we say about him will be less true than the reality of his life. His word, therefore, is *first* a narrative one in being itself the substance of the Christian proclamation, a historical reality that, because of resurrection, presses into the present and beyond and, in doing so, brings the story of Israel and the whole world into it. Although it sounds awkward, Jesus is, as the Word of God, the perfect incarnation of the being of Israel that God intended Israel to be. This is nothing less than his "fulfillment." (The law, after all, created a people to be one thing as opposed to another, initiating the story of Israel *as Israel*. Jesus is the fulfillment of this originary action of the law.)

A "receiving" Israel is a people who welcome God's story as their own, who side with God's action in taking their side over against the other nations. It is a people who take into their own life the sustaining effort of the God who made them a nation in the first place, to then be a people capable of recognizing words as God's. The crucial insight here presented, though, is that this is primarily a *narrative* presence of Word. Israel's ability to recognize Christ as God's Word among them is a skill that is only afforded by inhabiting a commensurate (indeed *the same*) story as the one that comes to it.

---

12. Ibid., 171.

Mary is the model for Israel (and as the church has recognized, a model for the church) in her reception of God's word by her *fiat mihi*: "*let it be to me* according to your word" (Luke 1:38). The incarnation was for Mary a word-presence of great intimacy and unmistakable consequence. Christ to her was every benefit that Israel might have received had it not so consistently refused God's word borne by the prophets. Mary receives God's word made flesh in her body, a readiness that the church quickly learned to admire and attempt to emulate in its common life and especially to reproduce in its sacramental life.[13] It is altogether fitting that Mary therefore genuinely embodies Israel's story as God's even while Israel herself, and as a whole, does not. Israel is consistently portrayed as a child born, not of fertility, but of the miracle of promise to barren conditions. Life promises to inhabit dry bones and lifeless wombs.

A christological hermeneutic, as I have been describing, is one way that theology inhabits what Rowan Williams calls the *communicative* mode: genuinely expecting to hear the truth from unexpected places. This is theology that takes seriously its task beyond the walls of universities and halls of study. As Williams describes it, such theology risks "experimenting with the rhetoric of its uncommitted environment."[14] It looks for the speaking and revelation of God from surprising sources and through unusual means. If the church is to reflect the unity of Christ who at great cost worked to make us one with each other, then the appropriate locus for the work of theology is within the churches. Such theology will strive to cultivate the dispositions necessary to call itself into question as it listens for the truth in what others are saying. "Looking for the grain of truth in every error, for the shadow of error in every truth, for the valid intention obscured in the false statement, and for the insight that has yet to be expressed—these are the practices necessary if the churches are to recover their visible unity in Christ."[15]

Likewise, Karl Barth repeatedly takes up this theme in his work, insisting that if the God who speaks through Scripture is the same God who is in Jesus Christ, then Christians must adopt commensurate ways of hearing.

---

13. Robert Jenson suggests that Mary ought to be seen as the "archprophet" since she brings forth the Word in her very person (*Canon and Creed*, 105).

14. Williams, *On Christian Theology*, xiv.

15. Hunsinger, *Eucharist and Ecumenism*, 21–22.

> Might not other human voices proclaim this Word too, and do they not do so by common experience? Does not God speak through *nature* too, through *history*, through Handel's "Largo" and all kinds of good *art*? And can we say that God does not speak directly to people today? No, we cannot, is the obvious answer.[16]

Yet this openness to hearing the truth from strangers is merely an aspect of the Christian's confidence that the gospel is true. It does not disparage the work of others when that work is not immediately relatable to the things the church has inherited. Nor does it assume that the ways Christianity has found to speak of divine things or things in God's world as God's are the final and complete ways to speak of them. Rather, theology in this mode rejoices in its middle-character, in the prospect and realization that it shares with Christ himself a historical existence that is most genuine the more it looks for ways to inhabit the truth it confesses. This is because inhabiting God's truth as creatures will, so long as it really is God's truth, always exceed every present formulation, every attempt to nail it down. The resurrection-reality of the church's present-tense existence is one that is lived in the lively, unpredictable, and surprising reality of Christ.

We should also recognize the way that this is a kind of listening that flows from the resurrection life of Jesus Christ rather than from other sources. The resurrection—as I argued in previous chapters—does not hold promise for the people who confess it as true other than through the kinds of things it now makes possible, what can now happen that could not happen before. And the things it makes possible is a very large set.

What then is the proper role for discernment, of deciding whether what we hear is in fact God speaking rather than something else? After all, not every generous overture directed toward Christianity's others ought to be an invitation altogether receptive to every disclosure. Not every unexpected contribution to the life of the world is a beneficent offering of the divine, awaiting discovery. Is there, in other words, in the risen life of Jesus a hermeneutical principle for distinguishing the one kind from the other?

The answer must almost always be no. In so answering, the church has traditionally prohibited any principle or code from doing the difficult work that the church reserves for itself, knowing that it does not simply

---

16. Barth, *Göttingen Dogmatics*, 33–34, emphasis original. Although I confess that I do not know why God is more likely to be found in good art rather than bad art unless so finding God is what accounts it as good, though that conclusion seems circular.

Theology and Surprise

fall to others to undertake it. Otherwise, such ways of answering the question of discernment threaten to render redundant the way that God has already spoken to and as the church itself, not primarily by way of giving it such prior standards for its judgment, but through its very birth as a people whose active life witnesses to God's life among mortals. The church tests the new speaking according to its Scriptures, to the apostolic witness, to the formation to which it entrusts its common life in liturgy and sacrament, and to the history of the saints' corroboration. None of these things speaks definitively or with finality even while they collectively direct the center of the church's life and confession around some things more than others. As a people who are extended throughout time and across the globe, the church does not have the luxury of assuming that whatever new thing God is now speaking is not somehow for the benefit of the whole church.

As important as I hope these reflections on the work of theology itself may be, even more important is to remember that there is no theology without theologians. The person of the theologian is subject to displaying aspects of her vocation—openness, closure, and intellectual rigor—that we may ultimately link to the manner of how she cultivates and responds to her love of God. The character of the theologian is not ancillary or incidental to the theology she produces because of the kind of discipline that theology is, with its unique object of study. In his 1919 essay "The Christian's Place in Society," Karl Barth discusses the difficulty of saying anything about God—that doing so is like trying to paint a bird in flight.[17] Our words will capture and nail God down. In response, Barth argues that theology ought to be forthcoming about its inherent inadequacy to the very project to which it devotes itself. It ought to engage in a dialectical approach, calling into question every claim with a commensurate, humble acknowledgment that affirming one thing of God at once also entails negations—not only of the opposites, but of the affirmations themselves. If God is a moving object, then theology names the struggle of our

---

17. "[O]ur position is really an instant in a *movement*, and any view of it is comparable to the momentary view of a bird in flight. Apart from the movement it is absolutely meaningless, incomprehensible, and impossible." Barth, *Word of God and the Word of Man*, 282–83, emphasis original.

words to keep up with the divine in its flux. What is therefore involved for the person of the theologian?

The Gospels clearly depict a Jesus who is always on the move, eluding the grasp of both his friends and enemies. In fact, we find that it is his followers and disciples who are most frequently needing to catch up to him. The gap between the one who forges ahead and the ones who stumble along behind increases as they near Jerusalem, the place of confrontation and death. The suggestion made here for the theologian is therefore not really new: theologians ought to strive to embody disciple-characteristics in their thinking of God-on-the-move by themselves being disciples of Jesus Christ. The reason is not necessarily that those who believe are more likely to speak truthfully about what they believe. It is that the process of believing in the Christian God revealed in Jesus Christ requires and imparts the appropriate dispositions for negotiating the otherness of God.

It is not clear that there are other ways whereby God (rather than idols) will be known, short of these disciplines of knowing. After all, God is himself the one who causes the need for disciples, though not primarily because in Christ God calls people to struggle with him by following behind. Rather, God causes disciples by being one who reveals himself to be knowable, albeit knowable through nonstandard means. Put differently, Christianity does not countenance a generalized concern for otherness, for the value of difference simply as such. Instead, it reckons with a God whose disclosure to us elicits a series of disciplines, comportments, attitudes, and modes of living oriented to the ambiguity of God's very self.

When theologians treat theology like the other disciplines—as primarily the study of ideas or texts or human behaviors—they cannot help contradicting the manner of their discipline's utter uniqueness. God *elicits* theological speech by being an antecedent communication to creation. God's consummate speech to the world *in* and *as* Christ is at once definitive and true, just as it is evasive and full of surprises.

Epilogue[1]

Texts: Exodus 24:12–18 * Matthew 17:1–9

One of the greatest gifts God has given to the life of worship is the Christian calendar. In observing it, we literally follow Jesus through his life. We are not casual onlookers of the manger at Christmas; we are the shepherds who cannot but praise God with the angelic hosts. We do not stand back while the wise men bring their gifts to the infant king; but Christ appears to us and looks at our hands—have we brought presents befitting a king or have we held back? We do not just observe Jesus being baptized by John in the Jordan River or calling disciples by the Sea of Galilee; we too must be baptized; and we are the ones being called. The story of Jesus is not only a historical one that we can survey from a comfortable distance. But it is a story that we share in as the church, the body of Christ. One of the most dramatic ways that we share in it is by structuring our lives around the rhythm of Christian worship. Each season in the church's calendar helps us grow.

So let's take stock of where we are. We have just come through Epiphany, that season in which we mark the appearances and manifestations of Christ among us. Typically, this is the time in which we rehearse the stories of the wise men, Jesus' baptism, and Jesus' presentation as a baby in the temple, fulfilling ancient prophecies. These are all Epiphany stories. What they all have in common and what Epiphany is all about: God showing himself to us. God making plain that this man, Jesus, is in fact the Son of God, the Messiah of Israel, the one promised of old to

1. A sermon preached on February 3, 2008, the Sunday after Epiphany.

bring deliverance and salvation, to release captives, to reign with justice and gentleness, and to bring a wayward people back to God. For us it is a period when we focus on who Jesus is, what we know about him, what we have been told, what others confess about him, and what we confess about him to others. It is a time of knowing.

But now Epiphany has passed. Where we are now is after that. Lent is fast approaching, but it is not yet upon us. This coming Wednesday, Ash Wednesday, will remind us of and enact for us our mortality in the imposition of ashes. But we are not there yet either. This morning, we find ourselves again in that awkward in-between stage called Ordinary Time. We are in between Epiphany and Lent, a veritable no-man's-land. This is a painful time of *not* knowing. It is a time of uncertainty. So, how do we live it?

If this were still Epiphany, we would know this God who appears to us, who makes himself known. But this Sunday, we are in the unpredictable presence of an elusive and mysterious God. We go out to meet him in the desert and he isn't there. We go up the mountain and there is only a cloud and silence. The voice may come, but it may not. And when it speaks, it says things that we do not understand and that we fundamentally do not want to hear.

This is the situation for Moses as he leaves behind the crowded valleys of Sinai and his fellow Israelites to ascend a mountain. God tells him to go up the mountain and wait. Wait. It is also this way for the disciples who follow Jesus up a different mountain, "apart" from the crowds. This is an appropriate Lenten image since Lent is a forty-day period of preparation that calls to mind the forty days that Jesus was tempted in the wilderness. Waiting can be the hardest thing because it marks out a period of indefinite duration in which we are powerless to bring about the thing we're waiting for. We may not even know what we are waiting for. It is unproductive time that only reminds us that there are nevertheless things we desperately need for which we are dependent on others.

Geographically, this places us at far remove from the places where things get done: the desert, mountains, wilderness. These images are almost entirely lost on us now. But for the ancient world, these are certainly not places of productivity—they are not even places of recreation as they are for us, but of danger and uncertainty. You did not ride Jeeps through the desert sands beyond the Jordan; you went there to die. You did not scale a mountain only to ski back to the lodge for breakfast and hot chocolate; you prepared to meet the unknown gods who ruled them, and you trembled with fear. Both of these readings this morning are haunted by the reality that these special places—desert places, mountain places—are places of the unknown. And yet they are the only places where we have a chance of meeting God in this strange time. The challenge for us is how we might live so unbearably out of control.

It seems that religious people have always scurried up mountains. The Stylites of Asia Minor in the fourth century are probably the most extreme example. Simeon Stylites climbed a pillar and didn't come back down until he died thirty-seven years later. Simeon was followed by other ascetics who sought time and space for contemplation, fasting, and the other spiritual disciplines. They spent years engrossed in prayer. Saint Alypius stood upright on a pillar for half a century until his legs gave out; but instead of coming back down, he lay on his side until his death fourteen years later. These hermits were not simply antisocial, but removed themselves from the bustle of everyday life for the sake of prayer and, ultimately, for the sake of those who could not do so. It became common for pilgrims to travel great distances and to ask for a word of wisdom from atop the pillars. Even emperors came, convinced that those who led lives of such devotion must have something worth saying.

It is easy for us to write off these practices as fanatical, even insane. It is true that they sought solitude in a very extreme way. But I suspect they would have considered our obsession with privacy to be no less insane. They sought solitude; we seek privacy. We seek privacy when we have something to hide or when we fear that who we really are has no acceptable public exterior. They sought solitude, however, in order to discover what is hidden and what they themselves might have hidden. These hermits teach us that we need not fear the depths.

It seems to me that solitude is an appropriate practice for us to consider as we head toward Lent, and on this morning in particular. In solitude, we confront the fact that there are no guarantees. Moses did not know how long he had to wait for something to happen. Come up the mountain and wait, God tells him. Unlike the lush, green fields that are continually nurturing seeds and promoting growth, the solitude the desert offers is much less certain. In Lent, we go to the desert to meet God, but we are not quite sure what we will find. We cannot know the God of the desert before going there. God is not a known quantity but a living being. If you ever find yourself following a known quantity into a future that is known ahead of time, it cannot be God you are following.

We need to be honest about how difficult all of this is for us. After all, we live in a society that encourages privacy and discourages solitude. Every individual is allowed to be their own tyrant. Just think about how private money is. We are terrified that someone will tell us what to do with it. Because it is *my* money. Well, guess what? It isn't your money; it's God's. What would it mean to be a people who know that everything we have is a gift and we must either give it back to God freely or live alienated from God? And how could we ever commit ourselves to the gospel's radical way of life unless at least some among us attempt it and show the rest of us how to do it? These ones will call us out of our privacy.

And yet we need to be clear that the Christian life is not a hedge against loneliness. We are not assured that laying our lives open before God will not get us hurt. We are only given the promise that we will not finally be left alone even in our loneliness. The challenge for us, made more acute as we enter Lent, is to be able to welcome God's presence in our midst by not insisting that we would rather be left alone. Our challenge is to reject the private and be open to how God will be present to us by risking the loneliness that solitude may bring.

Solitude takes patience. It risks loneliness. It embraces the wait. Moses waited six days before being called out of the cloud. He had no idea how long he needed to wait. How long do *we* need to wait? How long do we need to stop laboring and producing? How long before God acts? How long before God brings comfort to the parents who lose a child? How long before a friend can pick up from the fragments of a broken marriage and begin to live again? How long unemployed? How long estranged? We need to be honest that none of us knows the answer. All we can do is help one another practice patience as we wait. If we knew how long, we wouldn't need God; we would only need ourselves.

This is a season in which we are given permission to confront with honesty the fact that we do not really want God. For instance, we need Lent in order to prepare for the cross and resurrection of Jesus. We can't just find ourselves in the Garden one evening and expect that we will be faithful and stay by Jesus' side when the cops come. And we can't pretend that Jesus rising from the dead will just naturally make intuitive sense to us. It won't. There is a reason that among all of the Epiphany stories, the resurrection isn't one of them. Like the women who go there, we would go

Epilogue

to the tomb expecting to see something, hoping to have a complete picture of what we will find. But we will not find it. It is not there. It is gone.

And how could we ever think that that could possibly be good news? We need to be trained to seek after things that aren't there, to wait on a God who doesn't speak on cue—and to keep on waiting. We need to learn how to cope with a God who is as much an absence as a presence and how not to turn away from mysteries that we cannot know but that we desperately need.

The word Christians have for refusing privacy is *communion*. We therefore gather at this feast before us as a people that God has refused to let eat alone. Ironically, it is only in communion that we can risk solitude since we know we are never alone even when we are by ourselves. Solitude doesn't bring any guarantees with it. It doesn't submit to the predictability that we are addicted to in other areas of life. We are called to feast with one another on the body of Christ and so are built up *as that very body*. In doing so, we confess and demonstrate that we do not consume the Eucharist; it consumes us. It does not become our private possession but it dispossesses us. We do not draw it into our individual bodies. It draws us into it. It is not at our service; we are at its service.

This morning, God has refused our privacy by calling us into communion with himself and with one another. The time that we gather together in worship is not a private time. And this is particularly true of the next few moments. The sharing of the bread and cup is not a private transaction between you and God. It is public; it is laid open to those we eat with. And *only as such* is it open to God. This is a communal event because God's people are made God's people precisely by this event.

Yet this eminently public event does not protect us from the uncertainty to which we open ourselves by participating in it. And this is the long loneliness that Lent is for us. This bread and this cup are promises, not known quantities. They are mysteries before us because they are beyond our control. The solitude of the desert and the desolation of the mountaintop in which we meet God are still frightening even when, at long last, God speaks.

Therefore we may come to this table with trembling, aware that it has not been given to us to know the unknowable God in any other way than at great risk. What we hazard is the nearly impossible audacity to hold onto nothing other than the promises of a wild God. What we give up is our privacy as we yield up our efforts to grasp at certainty. What we receive is something we are not even sure we really want. But it is the only hope we have. Can we hope it? Can we want it? Can we believe it? Can we risk it? God help us.

Amen.

Bibliography

Adams, Nicholas. "Reasoning in Tradition." In *The Blackwell Companion to Christian Ethics*, edited by Stanley Hauerwas and Samuel Wells, 209–22. Blackwell Companions to Religion. Oxford: Blackwell, 2004.
Anselm. *Cur Deus Homo*. In *St. Anselm: Basic Writings*. Translated by S. N. Deane. La Salle, IL: Open Court, 1952.
Aristotle. *Nichomachean Ethics*. Translated by Terence Irwin. Indianapolis: Hackett, 1999.
Augustine, *Confessions*. Translated by Henry Chadwick. Oxford: Oxford University Press, 1998.
———. *De Trinitate*. Edited by John E. Rotelle. Translated by Edmund Hill. The Works of Saint Augustine: A Translation for the 21st Century 5. New York: New City, 1998.
———. *Sermon 43*. Translated by R. G. MacMullen. Nicene and Post-Nicene Fathers, First Series, 6. Edinburgh T. & T. Clark, 1988.
Avila, Rafael. *Worship and Politics*. Translated by Alan Neely. Maryknoll, NY: Orbis, 1981.
Balthasar, Hans Urs von. *Dare We Hope "That All Men Be Saved"? With a Short Discourse on Hell*. Translated by David Kipp and Lothar Krauth. San Francisco: Ignatius, 1986.
Barth, Karl. *Church Dogmatics*. 4 vols. Translated by G. W. Bromiley et al. Edinburgh: T. & T. Clark, 1956–1975.
———. *The Göttingen Dogmatics: Instruction in the Christian Religion*. Translated by Geoffrey W. Bromiley. Grand Rapids: Eerdmans, 1991.
———. *The Word of God and the Word of Man*. Translated by Douglas Horton. New York: Harper & Row, 1957.
Bauerschmidt, Frederick Christian. *Holy Teaching: Introducing the Summa Theologiae of St. Thomas Aquinas*. Grand Rapids: Brazos, 2005.
Borg, Marcus J., and N. T. Wright. *The Meaning of Jesus: Two Visions*. New York: HarperCollins, 1999.
Brooks, David. "The Power of Posterity." *The New York Times*, July 28, 2009. Online: http://www.nytimes.com/2009/07/28/opinion/28brooks.html.
Brown, Robert McAfee, editor. *The Essential Reinhold Niebuhr: Selected Essays and Addresses*. New Haven: Yale University Press, 1987.
Brueggemann, Walter. *Theology of the Old Testament: Testimony, Dispute, Advocacy*. Minneapolis: Fortress, 1997.
Calvin, John. *Institutes of the Christian Religion*. Edited by John T. McNeill. Translated by Ford Lewis Battles. Library of Christian Classics 20–21. London: SCM, 1960.

Bibliography

Cavanaugh, William T. *Migrations of the Holy: God, State, and the Political Meaning of the Church*. Grand Rapids: Eerdmans, 2011.

———. *Torture and Eucharist: Theology, Politics, and the Body of Christ*. Challenges in Contemporary Theology. Oxford: Blackwell, 1998.

Davies, Oliver, and Denys Turner, editors. *Silence and the Word: Negative Theology and Incarnation*. Cambridge: Cambridge University Press, 2002.

Davison, Andrew, editor. *Imaginative Apologetics: Theology, Philosophy and the Catholic Tradition*. London: SCM, 2011.

Eagleton, Terry. *Holy Terror*. Oxford: Oxford University Press, 2005.

———. *Ideology: An Introduction*. New York: Verso, 1991.

———, writing as Terence Eagleton. *The New Left Church*. London: Sheed & Ward, 1966.

Ellacuría, Ignacio, and Jon Sobrino, editors. *Mysterium Liberationis: Fundamental Concepts of Liberation Theology*. Maryknoll, NY: Orbis, 1993.

Gadamer, Hans-Georg. *Truth and Method*. Translation revised by Joel Weinsheimer and Donald G. Marshall. New York: Seabury, 1975.

Gregory of Nyssa. *Homilies on the Song of Songs*. In *From Glory to Glory: Texts from Gregory of Nyssa's Mystical Writings*. Translated and edited by Herbert Musurillo. Selected and introduced by Jean Daniélou. New York: Scribner, 1961.

Gunton, Colin, editor. *The Cambridge Companion to Christian Doctrine*. Cambridge Companions to Religion. Cambridge: Cambridge University Press, 1997.

Gutiérrez, Gustavo. "Option for the Poor." In *Mysterium Liberationis: Fundamental Concepts of Liberation Theology*, edited by Ignacio Ellacuría and Jon Sobrino, 235–50. Translated by Robert R. Barr. Maryknoll, NY: Orbis, 1993.

———. *A Theology of Liberation: History, Politics and Salvation*. Translated and edited by Sister Caridad Inda and John Eagleson. Maryknoll, NY: Orbis, 1973.

Hamilton, Edith, and Huntington Cairns, editors. *Plato: The Collected Dialogues*. Princeton: Princeton University Press, 1961.

Hart, David Bentley. *The Beauty of the Infinite: The Aesthetics of Christian Truth*. Grand Rapids: Eerdmands, 2003.

Hauerwas, Stanley. *Matthew*. Grand Rapids: Brazos, 2006.

Hauerwas, Stanley, and Samuel Wells, editors. *The Blackwell Companion to Christian Ethics*. Blackwell Companions to Religion. Oxford: Blackwell, 2004.

Hippolytus. *Appendix to the Works of Hippolytus*. In *Nicene and Post-Nicene Fathers*, vol. 5, edited by Philip Schaff. Edinburgh: T. & T. Clark, 1988.

Hollon, Bryan C. *Everything Is Sacred: Spiritual Exegesis in the Political Theology of Henri de Lubac*. Theopolitical Visions 3. Eugene, OR: Cascade Books, 2009.

Hovey, Craig. "Christian Ethics as Good News." In *Imaginative Apologetics: Theology, Philosophy and the Catholic Tradition*, edited by Andrew Davison, 98–111. London: SCM, 2011.

———. *To Share in the Body: A Theology of Martyrdom for Today's Church*. Grand Rapids: Brazos, 2008.

Hunsinger, George. *The Eucharist and Ecumenism: Let Us Keep the Feast*. Current Issues in Theology. Cambridge: Cambridge University Press, 2008.

Hurtado, Larry W. *Lord Jesus Christ: Devotion to Jesus in Earliest Christianity*. Grand Rapids: Eerdmans, 2003.

Janicaud, Dominique, et. al. *Phenomenology and the "Theological Turn": The French Debate*. Translated by Bernard G. Prusak, Jeffrey L. Kosky, and Thomas A. Carlson. Perspectives in Continental Philosophy. New York: Fordham University Press, 2002.

Jenson, Robert W. *Canon and Creed*. Louisville: Westminster John Knox, 2010.

———. "The Church and Sacraments." In *The Cambridge Companion to Christian Doctrine*, edited by Colin Gunton, 207–25. Cambridge Companions to Religion. Cambridge: Cambridge University Press, 1997.

———. *Ezekiel*. Grand Rapids: Brazos, 2009.

———. *Story and Promise: A Brief Theology of the Gospel about Jesus*. Philadelphia: Fortress, 1973.

———. *Systematic Theology*. Vol. 1, *The Triune God*. Oxford: Oxford University Press, 1997.

———. *Systematic Theology*. Vol. 2, *The Works of God*. Oxford: Oxford University Press, 1999.

Kirk, Kenneth. *The Vision of God: The Christian Doctrine of the Summum Bonum*. London: Longmans, Green, 1931.

Larsen, Timothy, and Daniel J. Treier, editors. *The Cambridge Companion to Evangelical Theology*. Cambridge Companions to Religion. Cambridge: Cambridge University Press, 2007.

Leithart, Peter J. *1 & 2 Kings*. Grand Rapids: Brazos, 2006.

Lohfink, Gerhard. *Does God Need the Church? Toward a Theology of the People of God*. Translated by Linda M. Maloney. Collegeville, MN: Liturgical, 1999.

Long, D. Stephen, and Tripp York. "Remembering: Offering Our Gifts." In *The Blackwell Companion to Christian Ethics*, edited by Stanley Hauerwas and Samuel Wells, 332–45. Blackwell Companions to Religion. Oxford: Blackwell, 2004.

Lubac, Henri de. *Corpus Mysticum: The Eucharist and the Church in the Middle Ages: A Historical Survey*. Translated by Gemma Simmonds with Richard Price and Christopher Stephens. Notre Dame: University of Notre Dame Press, 2006.

MacIntyre, Alasdair. "Epistemological Crises, Dramatic Narrative, and the Philosophy of Science." *Monist* 60.4 (1977) 453–72.

Malherbe, Abraham, and Everett Ferguson, editors and translators. *Gregory of Nyssa: The Life of Moses*. Classics of Western Spirituality. New York: Paulist, 1978.

Marion, Jean-Luc. *In Excess: Studies of Saturated Phenomena*. Translated by Robyn Horner and Vincent Berraud. Perspectives in Continental Philosophy. New York: Fordham University Press, 2002.

———. "The Saturated Phenomenon." In *Phenomenology and the "Theological Turn": The French Debate*, by Dominique Janicaud et al. Translated by Bernard G. Prusak, Jeffrey L. Kosky, and Thomas A. Carlson. New York: Fordham University Press, 2002.

Markus, Robert A. *Saeculum: History and Society in the Theology of St. Augustine*. Cambridge: Cambridge University Press, 1970.

McCabe, Herbert. *God Still Matters*. London: Continuum, 2002.

Milbank, John. "Can a Gift Be Given? Prolegomena to a Future Trinitarian Metaphysic." *Modern Theology* 11.1 (1995) 119–61.

———. *Theology and Social Theory: Beyond Secular Reason*. Oxford: Blackwell, 1990.

Moltmann, Jürgen. *The Church in the Power of the Spirit: A Contribution to Messianic Ecclesiology*. Translated by Margaret Kohl. London: SCM, 1977.

———. *Experiences of God*. Translated by Margaret Kohl. Minneapolis: Fortress, 1988.

———. *The Way of Jesus Christ: Christology in Messianic Dimensions*. Translated by Margaret Kohl. Minneapolis: Fortress, 1993.

Musurillo, Herbert, editor and translator. *From Glory to Glory: Texts from Gregory of Nyssa's Mystical Writings*. London: John Murray, 1961.

Bibliography

Nagel, Thomas. "Sexual Perversion." In *Theology and Sexuality: Classic and Contemporary Readings*, edited by Eugene F. Rogers Jr., 125–36. Blackwell Readings in Modern Theology. Malden, MA: Blackwell, 2002.

Niebuhr, Reinhold. "Augustine's Political Realism." In *The Essential Reinhold Niebuhr: Selected Essays and Addresses*, edited by Robert McAfee Brown, 123–41. New Haven: Yale University Press, 1987.

Nietzsche, Friedrich. *The Birth of Tragedy and the Genealogy of Morals*. Translated by Francis Golffing. Garden City, NY: Doubleday, 1956.

———. *The Gay Science*. Edited by Bernard Williams. Translated by Josefine Nauckhoff. Cambridge: Cambridge University Press, 2001.

———. "On Truth and Lies in a Nonmoral Sense." In *Philosophy and Truth: Selections from Nietzsche's Notebooks of the Early 1870s*, edited and translated by Daniel Breazeale, 79–97. Amherst, NY: Humanity, 1999.

———. *The Will to Power*. Edited by Walter Kaufmann. Translated by Walter Kaufmann and R. J. Hollingdale. New York: Vintage, 1968.

O'Donovan, Oliver. *The Desire of the Nations: Rediscovering the Roots of Political Theology*. Cambridge: Cambridge University Press, 2003.

Origen. *Commentary on Matthew*. Translated by John Patrick. Ante-Nicene Fathers 9. Edinburgh: T. & T. Clark, 1988.

Pickstock, Catherine. "Liturgy and Modernity." *Telos* 113 (1998) 19–40.

Placher, William C. *A History of Christian Theology: An Introduction*. Louisville: Westminster John Knox, 1983.

Plato. *Meno*. In *Plato: The Collected Dialogues*, edited by Edith Hamilton and Huntington Cairns, 353–84. Translated by W. K. C. Guthrie. Princeton: Princeton University Press, 1961.

———. *The Republic*. Translated by Richard W. Sterling and William C. Scott. New York: Norton, 1985.

Ratzinger, Joseph. *Jesus of Nazareth*. Vol. 1, *From the Baptism in the Jordan to the Transfiguration*. New York: Doubleday, 2007.

———. *Jesus of Nazareth*. Vol. 2, *Holy Week: From the Entrance into Jerusalem to the Resurrection*. San Francisco: Ignatius, 2011.

"Reservation of the Blessed Sacrament." In *The Catholic Encyclopedia*, edited by Charles George Herbermann et al., 12:784–85. New York: Encyclopedia Press, 1913.

Rogers, Eugene F., Jr., editor. *Theology and Sexuality: Classic and Contemporary Readings*. Blackwell Readings in Modern Theology. Malden, MA: Blackwell, 2002.

Sartre, Jean-Paul. *Being and Nothingness: An Essay on Phenomenological Ontology*. Translated by Hazel E. Barnes. New York: Philosophical Library, 1956.

Schmemann, Alexander. *For the Life of the World: Sacraments and Orthodoxy*. Crestwood, NY: St. Vladimir's Seminary Press, 1988.

Schwartz, Regina M. *Remembering and Repeating: On Milton's Theology and Poetics*. Chicago: University of Chicago Press, 1993.

Scott, Charles. *The Question of Ethics: Nietzsche, Foucault, Heidegger*. Indianapolis: Indiana University Press, 1990.

Sherwin, Byron L. *Faith Finding Meaning: A Theology of Judaism*. New York: Oxford University Press, 2009.

Sobrino, Jon. "Central Position of the Reign of God in Liberation Theology." In *Mysterium Liberationis: Fundamental Concepts of Liberation Theology*, edited by Ignacio Ellacuría and Jon Sobrino, 350–88. Maryknoll, NY: Orbis, 1993.

———. *The True Church and the Poor*. Translated by Matthew J. O'Connell. London: SCM, 1985.
Sugirtharajah, R. S. *Postcolonial Reconfigurations: An Alternative Way of Reading the Bible and Doing Theology*. London: SCM, 2003.
Thomas, Aquinas. *Disputed Questions on Virtue*. Translated by Ralph McInerny. South Bend, IN: St. Augustine's Press, 1999.
———. *Summa Theologica*. Translated by The Fathers of the English Dominican Province. Allen, TX: Christian Classics, 1981.
Treier, Daniel J. *Virtue and the Voice of God: Toward Theology as Wisdom*. Grand Rapids: Eerdmans, 2006.
Turner, Denys. "The Darkness of God and the Light of Christ: Negative Theology and Eucharistic Presence." *Modern Theology* 15.2 (1999) 143–58.
Webster, John. "Jesus Christ." In *The Cambridge Companion to Evangelical Theology*, edited by Timothy Larsen and Daniel J. Treier, 51–63. Cambridge Companions to Religion. Cambridge: Cambridge University Press, 2007.
Westphal, Merold. "Transfiguration as Saturated Phenomenon." *Journal of Philosophy and Scripture* 1.1 (2003) 26–35.
Williams, Rowan. *Arius: Heresy and Tradition*. Rev. ed. Grand Rapids: Eerdmans, 2002.
———. *Christ on Trial: How the Gospel Unsettles Our Judgment*. Grand Rapids: Eerdmans, 2000.
———. *On Christian Theology*. Oxford: Blackwell, 2000.
———. "The Politics of the Soul: A Reading of the City of God." *Milltown Studies* 19/20 (1987) 55–72.
Yoder, John Howard. *Body Politics: Five Practices of the Christian Community Before the Watching World*. Scottdale, PA: Herald, 1992.
———. *For the Nations: Essays Public and Evangelical*. Grand Rapids: Eerdmans, 1997.
———. *What Would You Do? A Serious Answer to a Standard Question*. Scottdale, PA: Herald, 1983.

Index

Abraham, 50, 109, 111–12, 128
absence, x, 7–8, 10, 15–16, 27, 151
Advent, 10, 22–24, 42–43, 45
Amos, 113–14
Anselm, 49, 75, 135
apologetics, 45, 91n14
Aquinas, Thomas, 4, 26, 71, 73, 85
Aristotle, 4, 6, 71, 72n7, 109
Arius, 65
ascension, 7, 45
Ash Wednesday, 148
Athanasius, 101, 139
atonement, 94, 135
Augustine, 5n4, 39–42, 64, 85, 95, 125, 138n3
autonomy, 79
Avila, Rafael, 123–24

Babel, 129
baptism, 73, 147
barrenness, 109–10, 143. *See also* children
Barth, Karl, 9n8, 39n16, 64n23, 109–10, 135, 143–45
Bauerschmidt, Frederick Christian, 74
Beckett, Samuel, 25
Bible, relation to tradition, 91–93, 135–36
Blumhart, Christoph, 117n5
boredom, 25, 31, 85n5
Brooks, David, 111–12
Brueggemann, Walter, 94n15

Bultmann, Rudolf, 59n14

Calvin, John, 46
Camus, Albert, 31, 42
capitalism, 138
Cavanaugh, William, 46, 129
charity, 43
children, 106–12
christology, 13, 52, 59, 83, 87
church, as body of Christ, 45–46, 50, 61–62, 116, 124–25, 127, 131, 147, 151; councils, 59, 140
Cohen, Will, 133n1
consumerism, 25, 108
convenientia, 71
Council of Toledo, 125n13
covenant, 3, 50, 76, 109, 111, 113–14, 128, 136, 142
creation, 33, 37, 48n28, 51, 62–67
creeds, 27n15, 56–57, 139–41
cross. *See* atonement
crucifixion (of Jesus), 70–73, 94
culture, 134, 137–38

Daniel, 43
David (king of Israel), 52, 115–16
Davies, Oliver, 27–28
Day of the Lord, 113–15
de Lubac, Henri, 124n11
Derrida, Jacques, 27n15
Didache, 129

Index

discernment, 144–45
discipleship, 82, 100, 105
dogma, 59–60
dreams (and fantasies), 32–34, 37–38, 53

Easter, 23–24
election, 74, 135
Elijah, 35
Éluard, Paul, 36
enemies, 47, 50, 69, 74n11, 100, 102–23, 116, 120, 137, 146
Epiphany, 147–48, 150
Eucharist, 10, 12, 15, 44–47, 56, 61–62, 122–29, 131, 137, 151; as sacrifice, 62, 123
exile / diaspora, 74, 129–30
Exodus, 134
Ezekiel, 114–16

Fall, the, 76–77, 80
Fanon, Frantz, 118
fate, 42
Florovsky, Georges, 139n6
forgiveness, 39n16, 96
Fout, Jason, x, 26n13, 74n11
freedom, 1, 23, 26n13, 41, 54n4, chapter 4 (69–81), 104–5, 108, 125, 138
friendship, chapter 6 (98–112)

Gadamer, Hans-Georg, 135–36
Gandhi, Mohandas, 47n26
gentiles, 50, 129, 137
gift, 4, 47–48, 61–68, 99, 102–3, 110, 128
God, name of God, 2
Good Friday, 93
Gregory of Nyssa, 8n7, 38, 133
Gutiérrez, Gustavo, 45n21, 107

Hamel, Johannes, 20–22
Hart, David Bentley, 10
harvest (scattering and gathering), 24, 43, 114, 128–32, 140
Hauerwas, Stanley, 39
Hegel, Georg W. F., 79
heresy, 141

hermeneutics, 89, 141, 143–44
Hippolytus, 122–23
Hollon, Bryan, 124n11
Holy Spirit, 12, 26n13, 45, 64, 68, 93
homoousios, 139

icons. *See* images
ideology, 37, 79, 138
idolatry, ix, 26, 49–50, 93, 146
images, 26, 29
incarnation, 33, chapter 3 (51–68), 83–86, 101, 118, 123, 141–43
injustice, 20, 115, 118–19. *See also* justice
innocence, 106–7
interpretation, 54; christological, 89, 116, 141–44
invisibility / visibility of the church, 38
Isaiah, 51–52, 116
Islam, 26
Israel, 70, 74, 109–10, 113–17, 128–31, 137, 141–43

Jenson, Robert W., 19n2, 29, 46, 56, 58n13, 59–60, 63, 83n1, 94–95, 141, 143n13
Jeremiah, 130
Jesus Christ, as judge, 24, 40, 46, 67, 113–18, 123; as king, 113–15, 117–22; death of, chapter 4 (69–81); return of, 7, 10, 24, 34, 36, 43–44, 67, 113, 113–15, 118–20, 129; two natures of, 13
John of Damascus, 26
John the Baptist, 43, 52
Jonah, 48–50, 131
Joseph (patriarch), 76
Judaism, 50, 111, 113
judgment / justice, 31, 39–42, 48–50, 52, 96, 113–23

Kant, Immanuel, 59n14, 79, 107
karma, 42, 113
Kingdom of God, 5, 35, 43–45, 56, 67, 107, 120, 122–23, 129

Index

kinship, 109
Kirk, Kenneth, 5
knowledge of God, ix, 1–9, 16, 20, 30, 49, 84–85, 118, 132, 133–35, 140–41, 144, 146, 148

Last Judgment, 40–41, 113, 116
Last Supper, 126–27
Law, 51, 117, 142
Lent, 22, 24, 148–51
liberation, 134
liturgy, 25, 27, 37n9, 43n19, 55–58, 60, 63–65, 86, 94n15, 137, 139–40, 145
Logos, 64, 81, 87
Lohfink, Gerhard 129
love, 14–15, 64, 85, 99–100, 102–3, 105, 116, 120–22, 145; of God, 74
Luther, Martin, 46

MacIntyre, Alasdair, 69n1
Marcion, 141
Marion, Jean-Luc, 19n3, 27n15
martyrdom, 21, 73–74, 96, 115, 123
Marxism, 138
Mary, 95, 118, 141, 143
Mauss, Marcell, 61n17. *See also* gift
McCabe, Herbert, 72–73, 78
memory/remembrance, 52, 55; in the Eucharist, 62, 126
Meno, 13–15, 17
mercy, 39–40, 49–50; acts and works of, 41–42, 120–21
Messiah, 35, 52, 70, 81, 83, 114, 116, 121, 137
Messianic hope, 52–53
"messianic secret," 83
Milbank, John, 61n17, 138n3
Milton, John, 55n6
miracles, 21, 63, 93, 123–24, 126, 128, 130, 143
modernism, x, 77, 79
Moltmann, Jürgen, 40, 117n5, 118
money, 43, 106–7, 119, 150
monophysitism, 101
monothelitism, 69

movement/motion, 3, 5–6, 130, 132, 145n17
mystery, 8, 23–25, 57, 62, 82–85, 105, 123, 131, 151. *See also* sacraments

Nagel, Thomas, 54
narrative, 56–57, 95–96, 127, 137, 141–42
necessity (cf Jesus Christ's death), 71–72, 75–77
negative / apophatic theology, 26–28
Nicea, 60, 67
Nicholl, Donald, 108
Niebuhr, Reinhold, 5n4
Nietzsche, Friedrich, 31–34, 36–37, 53–54, 69

O'Donovan, Oliver, 138
obedience, 23, 71–76, 80–81, 95, 104–5, 128, 142
Origen, 34, 120

parables, of Jesus, 38–39, 41
participation, 55, 60
patience, 4–7, 53, 82, 122, 125, 150
Paul, apostle, 22, 50, 71, 73, 91, 101, 107, 109n9, 117, 124–25, 131
peace, 90–91, 114
penal substitution (view of the atonement), 73
Pentecost, 12, 45, 67, 70, 76
Peter, 12, 35, 70, 76
Pickstock, Catherine, 37n9, 43n19, 55, 138n3
piety, 37
Plato, 5n3, 13–14
poor, the, 13, 39n16, 106, 107n5, 114, 119, 122
Pope John XXIII, 83n2
postmodernism, x, 28, 78–79, 84, 90
power, 73, 79, 93–94, 104–7, 117–19, 138
prayer, 11, 27, 56–58, 84, 86, 129, 149
preaching, 64n23, 67, 73
privacy, 54, 149–51
proclamation, 29, 58n13, 63–64, 66–67, 142

Index

profane, 36, 44
promise, 1–3, 15, 21, 29, 42, 50, 55, 73, 75, 88, 94, 96, 106, 109–12, 128
prophets, 43, 49n29, 51–52, 64, 86, 113, 115–16, 141–43
Psalms, 57n11

Radical Orthodoxy, 138n3
ransom, 74
Raphael, 33, 36–37
Ratzinger, Joseph, 89, 100n1
realism, Christian, 5n4
reason (and faith), 89–91
Reformation, 45, 62
resurrection, 61–67, 71–76, chapter 5 (82–97), 101–2, 116–17, 122–23, 126–32, 144, 150
rights, 110
ritual, 62, 86, 91. *See also* sacraments

sacraments, 12, 23, 36–37, 44–47, 61–62, 91, 93, 125–26, 128, 143
sacred, 36
salvation, 71–75, 96, 129
Sarah, 112
Sartre, Jean-Paul, 54n4
satisfactio, 74
saturated phenomenon, 19n3
"scandal of particularity," 58–59
Schmemann, Alexander, 36–37
Schwartz, Regina M., 55n6
Scott, Charles, 34n4
Second Vatican Council, 45, 83n2
secularism, 37, 137–38
seeing, 13, 33, 42, 53–54, 58, 61, 122
self-deception, 32
self-love, 64, 85, 94, 99
slavery, 134
sleep, chapter 2 (31–50)
Sobrino, Jon, 107n5, 119
socialism, 138
Socrates, 13–15, 17
solidarity, 51
solitude, 149–51
sterility, 111–12

strangers. *See* friendship
suffering, 7, 33, 35, 70–76, 86n8, 116, 118–19, 123. *See also* crucifixion
Sugirtharajah, R. S., 49n30

Taylor, Charles, 138n3
tradition, 140–41. *See also* Bible
Tran, Jonathan, 109n8
Transfiguration, 33–35, 37
Trent, Council of, 62n19
Trinity, 26n13, 59, 64, 66, 69, 141
truth, 22, 32, 38–39, 47–49, 53, 57, 59, 90–91, 143–44
Turner, Denys, 8n7, 27–28

unity, 124–27, 143
universal theology, 58–59

vindication, 93–96, 116
violence, 21, 48n27, 90–91, 93
virtues, 4–6, 47
von Speyr, Adrienne, 23
voyeurism, 53–55, 58, 61

waiting, chapter 1 (11–30), 39, 41, 45, 48–49, 53, 62, 82–85, 119–20, 123, 148, 151
weakness, 43, 114–15, 118–22
Webster, John, 87–89
Wesley, Charles, 11
Westphal, Merold, 35
will to truth, 32
Williams, Rowan, 28, 108, 139–40, 143
witness, 53, 59–61, 63–64, 67, 89–93, 142
Word of God, 63, 66, 116, 141–42,
worship, 5, 26, 64, 86, 91, 93, 131, 139, 147, 151. *See also* sacraments
wrath, of God, 96, 114
Wright, N. T., 69n2

Yoder, John Howard, 20–21, 47n26, 130, 131

Zwingli, Huldrych, 44, 126

www.ingramcontent.com/pod-product-compliance
Lightning Source LLC
Chambersburg PA
CBHW030858170426
43193CB00009BA/652